MEDALS & DECORATIONS OF THE THIRD REICH

(DIE AUSZEICHNUNGEN DES GROßDEUTSCHEN REICHS)

BADGES, DECORATIONS, INSIGNIA

(Orden, Ehrenzeichen, Abzeichen)

BY

DR. HEINRICH DOEHLE

Under State Secretary
in the Chancellery of the Head of State and State Chancellor

SS Colonel

Berlin 1943

Berlin Book and Periodical Press
E.O. Erdmenger & Co. K.G.

Comprehensive Editing and Thorough Translation into
English Text Provided
by
William E. Hamelman

Reprinted and Published by
REDDICK ENTERPRISES
P.O. Box 314
Denison, TX 75021
(903) 463-1366

Medals and Decorations of the Third Reich

(Die Auszeichnungen des Großdeutschen Reichs)

These writings are in the National Socialist Bibliography

Berlin, 25 January 1943.

The Chairman

of the Party Administrations Editing Commission

for the Protection of NS Writings

Originally produced by:
Printing: Gebr. Rath, Stuttgart, Friedrichstr. 13
Pictures and Klischees: Heußler & Co., Chemical Graphics Art Institute, Berlin SW 68
Award Ribbons: Carl Knoblauch, Silk Ribbon Factory, Berlin C 2

ISBN 0-9624883-4-8

Forward to the First Edition

As a result of a requirement for a concise work on all Orders and Decorations of the Third Reich, and because of the absence of one, I gladly obliged. In order to create a book which would be available to a greater number of people, it had to be kept short. Therefore, the numerous pre-war and wartime decorations and awards could only be done in condensed form without pictures.

My thanks go to the Braun House, the First SA Leadership, the High Command of the Armed Forces, the head of the Archive Staff of the State Ministry for Defense in Vienna, the State Ministry of the Interior, the State Labor Ministry, the leader of the State Sport Administration, the leadership of the State Youth Administration, the NSKK, the NSRK, and the State Society for Growth and Testing of German Pure Blood for their invaluable help in gathering this material.

Berlin, in May 1939 **The Author**

Forward to the Fourth Edition

The events of the war and the establishment of war decorations created the need for a new part of this book to illustrate these war awards. Furthermore, the war badges of the armed forces that were previously mentioned only in the appendix will be included in the first portion of this new edition.

At this time I would like to thank the State Ministers of Propaganda, who through their generous promotion made it possible, even in wartime, to print this edition in color.

As in the previous editions, we have included the new regulations as well as expanding the legal interpretation at the end of this book.

Berlin, in December 1942 **The Author**

Preface and Acknowledgments

The first edition of this original reference book of Third Reich awards was published in Berlin in 1939. It contained 88 pages and had only black and white photos of the awards. While the 1939 edition was an excellent source of the early awards, by 1943, a number of new war awards and decorations were established.

Dr. Doehle mentioned in the forward to the second edition that it was through the Propaganda Ministry that the 1943 edition contained award plates printed in color. The awards and decorations of the Third Reich were considered very important to the morale of the German soldier and the civilian population as well. Thus scarce resources and manpower were utilized in the production of such an in-depth study of the awards and decorations being given during the Third Reich period.

This is fortunate for today's collector and researcher as it has provided us complete and original source material, without the speculative conclusions found in other references. This translated version will stand on its merits through the years as the best source for the collector and researcher.

It includes virtually every military, political and civil decoration, medal, badge and award through December 1942. All illustrations are sharp, full scale photos reproduced exactly from the original publication. The addendum has been integrated into the text except for the Close Combat Badge and a couple of other entries. The decree, ordnance and regulation reference tables have been eliminated since they are unavailable.

Gau badges, Olympic awards, the Iron Cross and its various combinations, i.e. Oakleaves with Swords and Diamonds, as well as the Golden Party badge, Blood Order, German Cross in Gold, Long Service awards, and Battle Shields are all discussed in great detail. Also included are several campaign Cuff Titles, Army, Air Force and Navy badges, Honor Roll clasps and even several non-portable awards.

Reddick Enterprises is proud to add this outstanding work to our growing line of original source documentation and references. Most importantly, I would like to express my sincere appreciation to William E. Hamelman, first for his willingness to pursue the project and his dedication in seeing it through to fruition, and second for his flawless typesetting and layout, making the English translation almost perfectly identical to the original German version. His unique position as both a knowledgeable collector of militaria and German military historian, combined with his fluent command of the German language, make him one of only a few people capable of accomplishing such a superb translation.

We would like to express our sincere appreciation to Adrian Forman, Steven Wolfe and Neil Hardin.

J. Rex Reddick

Table of Contents

Pictures shown are in original size

Introduction

(Einleitung)

The Period Prior to the National Socialist Party

The Germany of 1871 until 1918 knew nothing of a national decoration. Although numerous decorations existed, they were of the various German States such as Prussia, Bavaria, Saxony, Württemberg, Baden, Hesse, and so on. The Emperor was known not as the "Emperor of the Germans," but as the King of Prussia and presided over the Association of German Princes and Kings *(Bundesfürsten)*and was so named the "German Emperor." William I in his capacity as emperor was responsible for the 1870/71 War Commemorative medal; William II instituted the 1901 China Medal, the 1907 Southwest African Campaign Medal, the 1912 Colonial Campaign Medal, and the 1918 Wound Badge. The institution and awarding of decorations by both Emperors was done only in the name of the "King of Prussia." This included, for example, the 1871 Ladies Merit Cross from March 22, 1871, the William Order from January 18, 1896 for Merit in working with the Health and Welfare Services, thc Red Cross Service Medal from October 1, 1898, and the General Honor Recognition Cross from January 27, 1900, the Prussian Crown Merit Order from January 18, 1901, the Iron Cross from August 5, 1914 and the Merit Cross for War Service from December 5, 1916. Because the Prussian decorations, especially the decorations for war, were awarded in large numbers to non-Prussians, they reached a grade and character that elevated them to the status of National Orders.This is especially true for the awarding of the Iron Cross, which in World War I was presented by the Emperor, as the supreme leader of all armed forces, to the armies of Prussia, Bavaria, Saxony, and Württemberg.

Since all 22 of the German Princes and Kings *(Bundesfürsten)* even the smallest, e.g., Waldeck, Reuss and Lippe, awarded their own Orders and decorations, the result was a colorful mixture of many different Orders and decorations of old Germany. In a pre-war publication on Orders and decorations of all countries of the world, the German Orders and decorations, with the exception of the Austrian, took up almost one-third of the book.

Every State reserved the right to approve or refuse its citizens permission to accept foreign honors and awards. This same right belonged to the German Emperor, although in accordance with the times and the way in which the States were organized, neither the State nor the Head of State needed to give permission for acceptance. Many more rights were in the hands of the individual States. For example, a Prussian who was decorated by the King of Bavaria was required to ask for permission to accept the decoration from the King of Prussia. Likewise if the King of Prussia wanted to decorate a citizen of Baden, the recipient had to obtain permission to accept the decoration from the Grand Duke of Baden. Even during World War I there was an example of a Württemberg citizen serving in a Prussian regiment who tried to get permission from the King of Würt-temberg before accepting the Iron Cross 2nd Class.

The Weimar Republic did not acknowledge any State awards or honors. It forbid any awarding of decorations from any State and ordered that no German citizen could accept any decorations or honors from any foreign countries.

This regulation was not always enforced; however, some awards were accepted from the Pope. This exception did not involve foreign Heads of State since the Pope did not own any land. *(The Vatican did not exist at the time).* The next award established was the Life Saving Medal *(on a ribbon)* which was accomplished in Prussia in 1925, and spread out to several other States. The Reconstruction Ministry introduced during 1922 the Colonial Medal *(the so-called Elephant Order)* for meritorious service in the colonies. As another example, on April 28, 1922 the requirements for the awarding of the Red Cross Merit Medal were changed to reflect its new status as an honor award. Thus it was no longer awarded by the State but was presented by the President of the German Red Cross. In addition, cities and provinces were allowed to present their own awards for honor and meritorious service, although these did not carry the value or status of State presentations.

Part One

General Legal Regulations

The Third Reich revised the Weimar Republic statutes over Titles, Orders and Decorations, as well as reinstating the acceptance of foreign distinguished awards. The first step was to establish the introduction of the awards of the Third Reich. This also transferred the authority for the presentation of the Life Saving Medal *(formerly awarded only by the president of the State)* away from the Council of States *(Landesregierungen)*. It could now only be awarded by Hitler.

The Council of States was, as during previous times, still allowed the exclusive right under the law to award the Loyal Service Award *(Treudienstabzeichen)*; however, this was amended on 7 April 1933. The acceptance of decorations no longer had to be approved by the state government or by its president. This shows the backward conditions in which thc National Socialist Party found itself after taking power.

According to the Statute of 30 January 1934, the official authority of the Council of States was transferred to the newly created Third Reich, effectively abolishing all rights by the Council of States to award any decorations. These rights, according to the supplemental Statute of 15 May 1934, had been completely changed. The design ordinance from 14 November 1935 along with the law of 1 July 1937, covering title, decorations and honors, was now given a new meaning. The regulation is now that the right to present awards and honors belongs primarily to the Führer and Reichs Chancellor. This regulation stated in Paragraph 3, Section 1 of the Statute of 1 July 1937 as follows:

> *"Orders and Decorations can only be bestowed by the Führer and Reichs Chancellor. Further decisions will belong only to the Führer and Reichs Chancellor."*

All previous rights of the Council of States in this area *(Loyal Service, Fire Protection, and Mining Service awards)* are abolished. A transfer from Hitler to subordinates of the right to make awards is possible only under extraordinary circumstances, such as during wartime; otherwise this practice was unauthorized.

This new ordinance did away with the growing number of post war decorations which were being worn, first abolishing state awards, and then the awards from other countries, associations and societies. For the most part, these were prohibited because of the proliferation of so many honors, medals, awards and decorations, some of which were considered to be of no value. As the result of this many badges were eliminated, such as the Langemarck Cross, the Border Protection and Free Corps unit badges awarded in commemoration of bravery in the field. The statute of 1 July 1937 specifies the awards and decorations that can still be worn. The wearing of all other facsimilies thereof is prohibited and the wearer shall be prosecuted.

Part Two

The Single Decorations

I. The State Orders and Decorations

A. War Decorations

1. The Honor Cross of the World War 1914/1918*

(Das Ehrenkreuz des Weltkriegs 1914/1918)

To commemorate the distinguished deeds of the German people during World War 1914/1918, the National President, General Field Marshal von Hindenburg, established through the Order of 13 July

Honor Cross for Combatants

Honor Cross for Non-Combatants

1934 the "Honor Cross for Participants in the World War 1914/1918" and for Next-of Kin. The Honor Cross was awarded in three forms:

for combatants
for non-combatants
for widows and parents of those who died in battle or as a result of wounds received in battle or having died in captivity or missing in action.

The cross was patterned after the reverse of the War Commemorative Medal of 1870/71.

* Incorrectly called the *"Hindenburg Cross."*

Honor Cross of Next-of-Kin

The Honor Cross awarded combatants *(Frontkämpferkreuz)* shows a laurel wreath circling the center medallion with the years "1914 1918." Crossed swords are between the arms , while the Honor Cross for Non-Combatants has no swords and has a wreath of oakleaves. Both crosses are bronze. The Honor Cross for Next-of-Kin is black. The Honor Cross is worn suspended from a ribbon with black edges, two white stripes and a center red stripe. The ribbon for the Honor Cross for Next-of-Kin is white edged, with two black stripes and a center red stripe.

The application for this award had a time limit, which has now expired and the acceptance of applications is now closed. The number of awards given:

for combatants		6 202 883
for non-combatants		1 120 449
for widows		345 132
for parents		372 950
	Total	8 041 414

By the decree of 30 November 1938, the State Minister of the Interior has introduced these awards into the OstMark and Sudeten German regions. The implementation for the awarding of this cross to war participants of German heritage from the east and west regions reclaimed by the Third Reich, is forthcoming. For attached military personnel outside these regions, the Führer, through the ordinance of 30 June 1942, has already ordered approval of these awards.

2. The Spanish Cross
(Das Spanien-Kreuz)

In recognition of the German volunteers who served in the Spanish Civil War and fought against Bolshevism, Hitler, by a decree dated 14 April 1939, established the Spanish Cross.

The Spanish Cross was awarded in Gold, Silver and Bronze Classes. The Gold Class was awarded only with swords. The Silver and Bronze Classes were awarded with and without swords. For outstanding bravery in combat, the Gold Class could be awarded with diamonds.

Spanish Cross in Gold with Diamonds

The badge consists of an eight pointed cross with a swastika in a center medallion. Between the arms of the cross is the Air Force eagle carrying a swastika. The Spanish Cross with Swords has the swords crossed through the center medallion with points up.

The Spanish Cross with Swords is awarded to the volunteers of the Condor Legion, as well as to crew members of German Naval ships in Spanish waters for the following actions:

a) Air attack off Ibiza
b) Bombardment of Almeria
c) Bombing raid of Palma

The Spanish Cross without Swords can be awarded to:

1) Courier flying personnel
2) Armed Forces personnel who served in Spain in the Condor Legion and also to Naval personnel who served a minimum of three months in Spanish waters.
3) German civilian personnel who served in the Condor Legion.

The Spanish Cross is worn on the right breast below the Blood Order. After the death of the recipient, the award remains with the next-of-kin.

The awards of the Spanish Cross have been completed and are:

8 462	Spanish Cross in Bronze with Swords
7 869	Spanish Cross in Bronze without Swords
8 304	Spanish Cross in Silver with Swords
327	Spanish Cross in Silver without Swords
1 126	Spanish Cross in Gold
28	Spanish Cross in Gold with Diamonds

3. The German Condor Legion Honor Cross for Next-of-Kin
(Das Ehrenkreuz für Hinterbliebene deutscher Spanienkämpfer)

To commemorate the heroic achievements in the effort to overthrow the Bolsheviks during the Spanish Civil War, Hitler established on 14 April 1939 the Condor Legion Honor Cross for Next-of-Kin. The cross is a smaller version of the Spanish Cross without Swords. It is bronze and suspended from a black ribbon with white-red-yellow-red edge stripes. The cross is worn on the left breast.

Condor Legion Honor Cross for Next-of-Kin

The Condor Legion Honor Cross for Next-of-Kin is awarded to the next-of-kin of German volunteers who

a) were killed in action
b) died in captivity
c) were missing in action
d) died as result of accidents
e) died of wounds received in action, accidently, or as the result of war-related sickness.

The entitlement to wear the Honor Cross is in the following order:

a) the widow
b) the oldest son, thereafter the daughter
c) the father, thereafter the mother
d) brother, thereafter the sister.

The awards of the Condor Legion Honor Cross for Next-of-Kin have been completed. A total of 315 Honor Crosses have been awarded.

4. The 1936-1939 Condor Legion Wound Badge

(Das Verwundetenabzeichen für deutsche Freiwillige im spanischen Freiheitskampf 1936/1939)

As a recognition for those German volunteers who fought the Bolsheviks in the Spanish Liberation War or those connected with the naval combat actions in Spanish waters by the German Navy and those who were wounded in action, Hitler on 22 May 1939 established the award of a 1936 Wound Badge.

Wound Badge for Condor Legion

The design of the badge is the same as those wound badges awarded during World War 1914-1918, but with the addition of a swastika to the center of the helmet. Depending on the severity of the wound or wounds, the badge is awarded in either black or silver.

The 1936 Wound Badge was worn on the left breast of the tunic. The awarding of the Condor Legion Wound Bage is closed (182 black badges and 1 silver were awarded).

5. The 1939 Iron Cross and the Clasps to the Iron Cross of World War 1914/1918

(Das Eiserne Kreus (1939) und die Spangen zum Eisernen Kreuz des Weltkrieges)

On 1 September 1939, the memorial day of the battle of Sedan,* the statutes of the Iron Cross, first established on 1 March 1813 by Prussian King Friedrich Wilhelm III in Breslau, were renewed. The Iron Cross statutes were also renewed during the wars of 1870 and 1914. The renewal statute begins:

> *"After my decision to call the German people to arms because of threatening attacks, I renew the Iron Cross, in memory of the heroic battles fought by the sons of Germany to protect the homeland in the earlier Great War."*

The renewal statutes of 1 September 1939 were supplemented on 3 June 1940.

The 1813, 1870 and 1914 Iron Cross was a Prussian award; however, the 1939 Iron Cross is a German award. Deviating from prior

* 1870-1871 Franco-German War

Left: Iron Cross 2nd Class
Below: Iron cross 1st Class

classification, the Iron Cross 1st and 2nd Class and Grand Cross of the Iron Cross *(the Blücher Star was not in the establishing document)* the 1939 Iron Cross will be awarded in seven grades, as follows:

Iron Cross 2nd Class
Iron Cross 1st Class
Knights Cross of the Iron Cross
Knights Cross of the Iron Cross with Oakleaves
Knights Cross of the Iron Cross with Oakleaves and Swords
Knights Cross of the Iron Cross with Oakleaves and Swords and Diamonds
Grand Cross of the Iron Cross

The original Iron Cross was designed by Karl Frederich Schinkel and retains its original form. The obverse shows in the center of the cross a swastika and in the lower arm the year 1939. The reverse shows in the bottom arm the year 1813. The suspension ribbon is black-white-red. The Knights Cross is a little larger than the 2nd Class and is worn at the throat. The Oakleaves to the Knights Cross is composed of three silver oak leaves added to the top arm of the cross and through which the suspension ribbon is threaded. The Grand Cross is twice the size of the Iron Cross 2nd Class and is worn at the throat on a wide black-white-red ribbon.

During the 1914-18 World War the Iron Cross was awarded in recognition of meritorious service in the front area on a black ribbon with white edge stripes, or on the home front mostly on the white ribbon with black edge stripes. During the 1914-18 World War the total number of awards were:

1 The Iron Cross on a golden breast star *(also called the Blücher Star")* awarded to General Field Marshal von Hindenburg.

5 Grand Cross of the Iron Cross *(awarded to Wilhelm II, Field Marshals von Hindenburg, von Mackensen and Prince Leopold of Bavaria, and General of Infantry Ludendorff).*

218 000	Iron Cross 1st Class
5 196 000	Iron Cross 2nd Class on the black-white *(combat)* ribbon
13 000	Iron Cross 2nd Class on the white-black (non-combat) ribbon.

The 1939 Iron Cross is awarded only for bravery in combat action and for meritorious troop leadership. In the awarding of the Grand Cross of the Iron Cross, Hitler reserved the right to award this Grand Cross only for the most outstanding results of decisions affecting the outcome of the war. Hitler presented the Grand Cross of the Iron Cross

Knights Cross of the Iron Cross

Knights Cross of the Iron Cross with Oakleaves

to the commander-in chief of the Air Force, Hermann Göring, on 19 July 1940 at the Reichstag and at the same time promoted Göring to Reichs Marshal of the Third Reich. On 15 July 1941 the Oakleaves with Swords and Diamonds, the highest German bravery decoration, was presented by Hitler for the first time to Colonel Werner Mölders for downing 101 enemy aircraft during this war and making a total of 115 including the victories during the Spanish Civil War.

Oakleaves with Swords to the Knights Cross of the Iron Cross

Awards made through 1 January 1943 to Armed Forces Personnel:

Oakleaves with Swords and Diamonds	5
Oakleaves with Swords	23
Oakleaves	168
Knights Cross of the Iron Cross	2 237

Knights Cross of the Iron Cross with Oakleaves with Swords and Diamonds

If the recipient of the 1939 Iron Cross has been decorated with one or both classes of the Iron Cross of World War 1914/1918, he will then receive a silver clasp showing the National Eagle with the year 1939. The clasp to the Iron Cross 2nd Class will be worn attached to a ribbon in the buttonhole. The 1939 1st Class clasp will be worn attached to the tunic above the 1914 Iron Cross 1st Class.

The 1st and 2nd Class and the clasps will be awarded in the name of Hitler through the commanders of the three branches of the Armed Forces or by the Supreme Commander of the Armed Forces. The commanders-in-chief are permitted to delegate award authority to division commanders and commanders of smaller units.

The presentation of the Knights Cross of the Iron Cross, the Oakleaves and the Grand Cross of the Iron Cross will be done only by Hitler.

Grand Cross of the Iron Cross

The awarding of the Iron Cross and the Clasps are at the discretion of the Chancellery of the Führer and through requests of the High Command of the armed forces.

The award documents for the Iron Cross 1st and 2nd Classes are given in the name of Hitler and the Chief of the Supreme High Command of the armed forces and are written at the place of presentation. The presentation document for the Knights Cross, for the Oakleaves to the Knights Cross, for the Oakleaves with Swords to the Knights Cross, Oakleaves with Swords and Diamonds to the Knights Cross, as well as the Grand Cross of the Knights Cross is made of parchment in a special leather cover *(designed by Mrs. Troost, Munich)* and each is signed by Hitler

In general, foreigners will not be awarded the Iron Cross. Members of the armed forces of allied countries can receive the Iron Cross for exceptional bravery and outstanding leadership while under the command of the German armed forces. This is considered as co-operation with the German armed forces. The Iron Cross can also be awarded to foreign volunteers under oath to the Führer and who fought in the German armed forces against the Soviet Union. They can also be awarded the War Merit Cross *(see page 25)* otherwise the decoration for members of the armed forces of allied countries is the Merit medal of the German Eagle Order with or without swords *(see page 45)*. On several special occasions the Führer awarded the Iron Cross to statesmen and high officers of countries allied to Germany.

6. The 1939 Wound Badge

Das Verwundetenabzeichen (1939)

To recognize and honor those individuals who risked their lives for the Fatherland in combat with the enemy and were wounded or crippled, Hitler established by statute on 1 September 1939 a Wound Badge in three classes:

in Black for 1st - 2nd wounds
in Silver for 3rd - 4th wounds
in Gold for 5th or more wounds
} Wounding or Crippling

Earlier wounds for which the World War 1914/1918 Wound Badge has been awarded will be counted towards the next higher class.

The badge, like the 1936/1939 Condor Legion Wound Badge will show the swastika on the helmet. The badge will be worn on the left side of the tunic.

1939 Wound Badge

According to the regulations for the awarding of the 1939 Wound Badge from the commander-in-chief of the armed forces, the silver class of the wound badge can be awarded without consideration of the number of wounds received. The silver class would be given when the wound is the loss of a hand or foot, loss of an eye or hearing or partial loss of hearing. The 1939 Silver Wound Badge can also be awarded for brain damage and/or facial disfigurement. The golden class of the 1939 Wound Badge can also be awarded without consideration of the number of wounds received providing the wounded person has one or more of the above mentioned wounds and already has the silver class.

The 1939 Gold Wound Badge can also be awarded if the wound caused total blindness or severe brain damage which must require constant care. Any unique wounding can obtain a higher class of the wound badge providing the higher class is properly requested through channels to the commander-in-chief of the armed forces.

The awarding of the 1939 Wound Badge goes through the proper military channels starting with the battalion commanders on up. in the case of an emergency, the medical facility where the wounded person is under care can initiate the awarding process of the wound badge by informing the individual's company.

The recipient of the wound badge will receive a certificate. The award will then be recorded in the serviceman's record book, in the pass book and the military records section as well as in the rank list.

The 1939 Wound Badge is awarded not only to military personnel but also to individuals being wounded or crippled through enemy action. It can also be awarded to police officers, members of the Organization Todt, Workers Service *(Arbeitsdienst)*, Air Raid Protection Service *(Luftschutzdienst)*, members of the NSDAP, and to individuals working with the armed forces or under orders of military jurisdiction who have been wounded during air raids.

7. The War Merit Cross

(Das Kriegsverdienstkreus)

Created on 18 October 1939, to commemorate the victory at the battle of Leipzig, Hitler established this award in recognition of war merit during this war. The new award statutes were patterned after the Iron Cross. The statutes were further expanded on 19 August 1940 and 28 September 1941.

The War Merit Cross is awarded in the following levels:

War Merit Cross 2nd Class
War Merit Cross 1st Class
Knights Cross of the War Merit Cross

The decoration is given with and without swords. Also, a War Merit Medal is awarded.

War Merit Cross

2nd Class with Swords

2nd Class without Swords

The award insignia is an eight pointed cross with a round center medallion showing a swastika surrounded by an oakleaf wreath. The reverse medallion of the War Merit Cross 2nd Class and the Knights Cross of the War Merit Cross shows the year "1939." The 2nd Class of the War Merit Cross is bronze, the 1st Class is silver. The Knights Cross is silver and larger than the War Merit Cross 2nd Class. The War Merit Medal is bronze and the obverse shows an eight pointed

War Merit Cross

1st Class with Swords

1st Class without Swords

cross in the form of the War Merit Cross. On the reverse is the inscription "For War Merit 1939" (designed by Prof. Richard Klein, Munich).

The 2nd Class of the War Merit Cross is worn suspended from a ribbon when worn with a group or through the second buttonhole of the uniform tunic. The ribbon has a black middle stripe and on each side a narrow white and red stripe. When worn from a group the War Merit Cross 2nd Class (with or without swords) is worn following the 1914 Iron Cross 2nd Class, but preceding the sword awards of World War 1. The ribbon of the War Merit Cross 2nd Class with Swords is worn in the buttonhole of the tunic *without* the sword attachment. When worn on the ribbon bar, the swords will be bronze.

The War Merit Cross 1st Class is worn without ribbon on the left side of the tunic below the 1914 Iron Cross 1st Class.

The Knights Cross of the War Merit Cross is worn from a wide ribbon around the neck.

The War Merit Medal is suspended from a ribbon when worn with a group or from the second buttonhole of the military tunic. The ribbon is the same as for the War Merit Cross 2nd Class except that the ribbon has a small red center stripe.

The War Merit Cross is awarded with Swords for meritorious action under enemy fire or combat activities. The War Merit Cross without Swords is awarded for meritorious service without being directly under enemy fire.

War Merit Medal

The awarding of each class of the War Merit Cross is given solely on the basis of merit and not of service rank or service posi-tion.To receive the award of the War Merit Cross 1st Class without having received the War Merit Cross 2nd Class is limited to outstanding meritorious service only. In such cases, the War Merit Cross 2nd Class can be awarded with the War Merit Cross 1st Class. The award of the War Merit Cross with swords is the higher award of the War Merit Cross.

If the War Merit Cross with Swords is awarded to a recipient of the War Merit Cross without Swords, only the War Merit Cross with Swords will be worn. The War Merit Cross without Swords will remain in the possession of the recipient. The regulation stating that the recipient of the Iron Cross or the 1939 Clasp to the 1914 Iron Cross cannot be awarded the War Merit Cross has been revoked as of September 28, 1941.

The awarding of the Knights Cross of the War Merit Cross will be done personally by Hitler. The awarding of the War Merit Cross to soldiers, government officials, armed forces administrators and non-armed forces civil personnel will be done in the name of Hitler and/or the highest commanders-in-chief of all branches of the military forces. Civilians receiving the award will be recommended through state ministers or the Presidential chancellery and will be decided by Hitler.

Knights Cross of the War Merit Cross with Swords

For the awarding of the War Merit Cross with Swords, it shall be authorized by the commander-in-chief of the armed forces. For merit by members of the Air Defense personnel and non-military Air Defense personnel, the award of the War Merit Cross without Swords will be approved by the Air Defense Ministry. The award of the War Merit Cross with Swords to Air Force personnel will be authorized through the commander-in-chief of the Air Force (*Luftwaffe*).

The War Merit Cross and the War Merit Medal basically will not be awarded to foreigners, with the exception of foreign volunteers ser-ving in the German armed forces against the Soviet Union. These foreign volunteers will be decorated the same as or equal to the German soldier in the military forces.

Knights Cross of the War Merit Cross without Swords

Through the request of Dr. Ley, Chief of State Organization, and the Secretary of State for Weapons and Munitions, Professor Speer, Hitler permitted the creation of an "Outstanding War Factory Classification." The War Merit Cross will be awarded in recognition of outstanding war production in both performance and teamwork. The factory team being recognized shall receive a certificate authorizing the right to display the War Merit Cross on a banner.

8. The German Cross
(Das Deutsches Kreuz)

On September 28, 1941, Hitler established the War Order of the German Cross. This decoration is an armed forces decoration. The award is given in a gold and a silver class. The badge consists of an eight pointed, dark gray, silver edged star 65 mm in diameter, a black

The German Cross in Gold

silver-edged swastika is attached to a matt-silver medallion. This is surrounded by a laurel leaves wreath with the year "1941" at the bottom. The German Cross is worn on the right pocket of the military tunic. (see addendum No. 1, page 151)

The German Cross in gold is awarded in recognition of multiple acts of outstanding bravery or distinguished leadership. The German Cross in silver is awarded in recognition of distinguished achievements in completion of military missions. Criteria for the awarding of the German Cross in gold or silver is to have received the 1939 Iron Cross 1st Class or the 1939 Clasp to the 1914 Iron Cross or the War Merit Cross 1st Class with Swords.

The recipient also receives an authorization document.

As a special recognition, Hitler reserves the right to award the German Cross with Diamonds.

The recipient will receive a special authorization document which will be similar to that given to recipients of the Knights Cross of the Iron Cross.

The German Cross can also be worn as an embroidered insignia.

9. 1941/42 Eastern Winter Campaign Medal

(Die Medaille "Winterschlacht im Osten 1941/42" [Ostmedaille])

To honor the heroic campaigns against the Bolshevik enemy during the winter of 1941/42, Hitler established on May 26, 1942 the "Eastern Winter Campaign Medal." The medal was designed by SS Sergeant Ernst Krause. The medal is worn suspended from a ribbon when worn with a group or through the second buttonhole of the military tunic after the Iron Cross and War Merit Cross. The ribbon is red with a narrow center stripe of white/black/white.

Eastern Winter Campaign Medal

The Eastern Winter Campaign Medal is awarded in recognition of having fought against the Bolshevik enemy during the Russian winter between November 15, 1941 and April 15, 1942. The criteria for the award of the Eastern Winter Campaign Medal is:

a) a minimum of 14 days participation in combat.
For Air Force flying personnel participation in a minimum of 30 combat missions

or b) Receiving wounds or frostbite which qualified for the Wound Badge.

or c) 60 days uninterupted service in the combat zone.

The preceding conditions must have been met in the period between November 15, 1941 and April 15, 1942 (both days included) and in the area of operations under the armed forces commander of the Ukraine and eastward or in the area of operations of Finnland eastward to the Russo-Finnish border of 1940.

The criteria for award:

a) for military and non-military personnel under the jurisdiction of the armed forces or attached thereto.
By commanders of regiments, commanders of independent battalions upwards and so on.

b) for personnel in allied and foreign forces.
   awarded by regimental and battalion commanders equivalant to the German armed forces.

c) patients confined to a military hospital.
   authorized by the hospital commander.

d) for all other non-military personnel serving in the previously mentioned areas.
   through the authorization of the proper ministries.

The recipient will receive an authorization document. The award will also be recorded in the recipient's service records.

The Eastern Winter Campaign Medal will be awarded to those meeting the following criteria:

a) Killed in action.
b) Military personnel of allied forces under the command of the German armed forces.
c) Foreign volunteers serving in the German armed forces.
d) Subjects of foreign nations liberated from the Bolshevik area.

The Eastern Winter Campaign Medal can also be given to women and foreigners for service.

10. Swords on Peace Decorations

(Schwerter zu Friedensauszeichnungen)

Several State orders and decorations that are usually awarded during peace time can be awarded with swords when authorized by Hitler during this war as a special recognition of war service. This is in regard to orders and decorations specifically designed to be awarded only to foreigners, such as the German Eagle Merit Order. Also Spanish and Italian military personnel having served during the Spanish campaign can receive swords on merit awards and the German Social Service Medal.

B. Peace Decorations

(Friedensauszeichnungen)

1. The German Olympic Merit Decoration and the German Olympic Commemorative Medal

(Das Deutsche Olympia-Ehrenzeichen - Deutsche Olympia-Erinnerungsmedaille)

The XI Olympic games were held in Berlin during the summer of 1936 and the Olympic winter games held in Garmisch-Partenkirchen during February 1936. Hitler established on February 4, 1936 the sta-

Olympic Merit Decoration 1st Class

tutes creating the German Olympic Merit Decoration. The decoration is awarded through the recommendation of the Ministry of the Interior.

The Olympic Merit Decoration *(designed by Prof. Waldemar Raemisch)* is a 10 pointed star composed of five straight white enameled arms with golden edges ending in two points, one arm points downward. This is set atop five golden ridged arms with straight ends. Across the center of the star is the five enameled Olympic rings with golden edges. One golden ridged arm points upward to which is attached the national eagle in white enamel with a golden edge. To the reverse of the head of the eagle is attached a small golden ring through which a large three ridged vertical golden ring is attached. The 1st Class badge is suspended from a neck ribbon 5 cm wide, brick red with black edges and with five narrow white stripes in the center.

The 2nd Class decoration is in the same form as the 1st Class except smaller. It is worn suspended from a 3 cm wide ribbon on the left breast.

The 1st Class was awarded for outstanding leadership in the organization of the games. The 2nd Class was awarded in recognition of distinguished service during the games. Because of the large numbers of persons involved in the games who did not meet the criteria to receive either the 1st or 2nd Class, and through the request of the Ministry of the Interior, Hitler authorized the German Olympic Commemorative Medal on July 31, 1936.

The Olympic decorations and medals were awarded to Germans and foreign nationals. Judging by the numbers requested, the medal was very highly regarded by foreign countries.

The 1st Class was awarded to 767 persons, the 2nd Class to 3364, and the German Olympic Commemorative Medal was given to a total of 54,915 individuals. The Orders Chancellory recorded all awards.

Top:
Olympic Merit Decoration 2nd Class

Below:
Olympic Commemorative Medal

2. The German National Order for Art and Science

(Der Deutsche Nationalorden für Kunst und Wissenschaft)

Through statutes of January 30, 1937, Hitler established the German National Prize for Art and Science. The awarding of the Nobel Prize to German writer Karl von Ossietzky, condemned for high treason, made us reevaluate the way we looked upon the Nobel Prize community in order to ensure that such an awarding would not happen in the future. Therefore, Hitler created the German National Prize for Art and Science and forbid the acceptance of the Nobel Prize by any German citizen.

The Prize is to be awarded each year to three outstanding German citizens who will receive 100,000.00 RM which will be equally divided. The conferring of the award will take place annually at the anniversary of the establishment of the NSDAP. The award will be requested by the

Star of the German National Order for Art and Science

Ministry of Information and Propaganda. Along with the Prize money the recipient also receives the German National Order for Art and Science with a certificate.

The Order, a round four pointed platinum star, with four gold National Eagles attached (designed by sculptor Müller-Erfurt, Berlin) is worn on the left breast. In the center is a medallion with a red enameled center with the gold head of Pallas Athene. On an ivory colored enameled background in gold letters is the inscription "For Art and Science." This is surrounded by diamonds set in a gold border. The diameter of the star from point to point is 9.6 centimeters. The sash measures 10.5 centimeters and is worn from the right shoulder to the left hip and is red with white edge stripes and a red border. In the center of the rosette is an embroidered National Eagle. The rosette is placed over the crossed ends of the sash.

The German National Prize for Art and Science is the highest peace decoration. It was awarded for the first time in 1937 by Hitler to the deceased architect Professor Ludwig Troost to recognize his outstanding contributions to Germany.

Hitler also authorized in 1937 the following awards:

1. State Leader *(Reichsleiter)* Alfred Rosenberg
2. the monetary award to be equally divided:
   a) Privy Councillor *(Geheimrat)* Professor Dr. August Bier and
   b) Privy Councillor *(Geheimrat)* Professor Dr. Ferdinand Sauerbruch
3. Professor Dr. Wilhelm Filchner

In 1938 the recipients of the National Prize for Art and Science were:

1. General Inspector of the German Highway System, Dr. Engineer Fritz Todt
2. Designer and Builder of the Volkswagen, Professor Dr. Engineer Ferdinand Porsche
3. the monetary award to be equally divided:
   a) Professor Dr.-Engineer Dr. philosophy Ernst Heinkel and
   b) Professor Diplomate Engineer Willy Messerschmitt

The award included the star and sash.

Opposite page: The sash of the German National Order for Art and Science (shown approximately one-third size).

Star of the Grand Cross of the German Eagle Order in Gold

3. The German Eagle Order

Der Deutsche Adlerorden

The lack of German decorations available to foreigners was resulting in an inequity in the political-diplomatic circles with other foreign governments. Hitler ordered that an award be created that could be given to foreigners. On May 1, 1937 an Order to be awarded only to foreigners was authorized. It was called the "German Eagle Order" *(actually the official name is the "Merit Order of the German Eagle").* This Order was comparable to International Orders. The classes are:

Grand Cross (shoulder sash with breast star)
Grand Commander/Grand Officer (neck badge with breast star)
Commander (neck badge)
Officer (pinback badge or special badge for wear on a group)
Knight (for wear on a group)

Opposite page: Grand Cross of the German Eagle Order in Gold (2/3 size)

Grand Cross of the German Eagle Order (2/3 size)

Star of the Grand Cross of the German Eagle Order

The Order as the German Foreign Order was subdivided into five levels:

1. "Grand Cross of the German Eagle Order" (shoulder sash with eight pointed breast star)
2. "German Eagle Order with Star" (neck badge with six pointed breast star)
3. "German Eagle Order 1st Level" (neck badge)
4. "German Eagle Order 2nd Level" (pinback badge)
5. "German Eagle Order 3rd Level" (suspended from ribbon)

For meritorious service to the German State, a "German Merit Medal" was authorized.

On April 20, 1939, Hitler established a special high decoration called 'Gold Grand Cross of the German Eagle Order." The maximum number of awards of this special class of the German Eagle Order will be limited to 16. This special class has been awarded to:

1. Italian Minister of Foreign Affairs Count Galeazzo Ciano de Cortellazzo.

2. Spanish Chief-of-State and Generalissimo, Francisco Franco Bahamonde
3. King of Bulgaria, Boris III
4. State Administrator of the Kingdom of Hungary, Admiral Nickolaus Horthy von Nagybanya
5. State President of Finland, Risto Heikki Ryti.
6. State Prime Minister of Rumania, Marshall Jon Antonescu

German Eagle Order 1st Level

Note: The following pictures of the Grand Cross, the 1st, 2nd, and 3rd Levels are shown without Swords. The awards with swords are shown on the opposite page.

Opposite page: German Eagle Order with Star and Swords

Above:
German Eagle Order 2nd Level

Right:
German Eagle Order 3rd Level

7. Japanese Ambassador in Berlin, Lt. General Hiroshi Oshima
8. Commander-in-Chief of the Finnish Armed Forces, Field Marshal Baron Carl Gustaf Mannerheim

The Italian Chief-of-State and Duce Benito Mussolini was decorated by Hitler with the Grand Cross of the German Eagle Order in Gold with Diamonds on September 25, 1937.

The statutes dated April 20, 1939 state that in recognition of distinguished military merit, the German Eagle Order can be awarded with Swords.

The badge of the Order is an eight pointed, white enameled gold edged cross. Between the arms of the cross a gold German eagle holding a gold white enameled oakleaves wreath with a gold swastika in the center (designed by Professor Richard Klein, Munich).

The ribbon of the Order is red with narrow white-black-white edge stripes.

The Grand Cross in gold has a width of 66 mm and is suspended from a 100 mm sash worn from the right shoulder to the left hip. Also worn with this is a gold eight-pointed rayed breast star measuring 91 mm wide. The badge to the Order is 47 mm and set on the center of the star. The breast star is worn on left side of the tunic. The Grand Cross

German Merit Medal

without Swords *with Swords*

in silver is 60 mm wide and is worn with a silver breast star that is 80 mm wide. The red of the ribbon of the Grand Cross in gold is somewhat darker than the normal suspension ribbon. The edge stripes are also wider.

Regarding the other classes, reference is made to the pictured awards.

The German Eagle Order was to be awarded only to foreigners. On special occasions the Minister of Foreign Affairs and the National Administrator of Bohemia and Moravia wear a special class of this Order.

The awarding of the Order follows the request of the Ministry of Foreign Affairs for approval by Hitler which is then forwarded to the Secretary of State. With the completion of the documentation for the award, the authorization is forwarded to the Office of Foreign Affairs which in turn contacts the embassy. The ambassador then delivers the decoration to the recipient.

4. Military Service Awards and Civil Service Honor Awards

Die Dienstauszeichnung und Treudienst-Ehrenzeichen

The Military Service and the Civil Service Honor Awards are worn suspended from a corn flower blue ribbon.

a) The Service Awards of the Armed Forces

In keeping with the tradition of the old armed forces, Hitler authorized, on March 16, 1936, the reinstatement of the general draft, and the Service Awards of the Armed Forces. The award was given in four classes.

4 years service — matt silver medal
12 years service — bronze medal
18 years service — silver cross
25 years service — golden cross

The medal for the 4th and 3rd class has on the obverse the Armed Forces Eagle surrounded by the inscription "Loyal Service in the Armed Forces." On the reverse are the numbers 4 or 12 enclosed within a wreath of oakleaves. The 2nd and 1st Class cross has in the obverse medallion the Armed Forces Eagle and in the reverse medallion the numbers 18 or 25. The 1st Class cross is somewhat larger than the 2nd Class cross *(designed by Professor Richard Klein, Munich)*.

Service Award of the Armed Forces 4th Class (for 4 years service)

Reverse

On the ribbon is the Armed Forces Eagle for Army and Navy

Service Award of the Armed Forces

3rd Class (for 12 years service)

On the ribbon is the Eagle for the Luftwaffe

2nd Class (for 18 years service)

On the ribbon is the Eagle for Army and Navy

Service Award of the Armed Forces 1st Class (for 25 years service)
with oakleaves for 40 years service

Reverse

The metal Eagle of the Armed Forces attached to the ribbon is the same color as the respective branch of service to which the recipient is serving or has served.

After the awarding of the higher class, the lower class can be also worn as indicated:

3rd Class worn with the 4th Class
2nd Class worn with the 4th Class
1st Class worn with the 3rd Class

In recognition of 40 years service in the armed forces, Hitler authorized a wreath of oakleaves to be worn on the 25 year service award. It was worn on the ribbon below the National Eagle of the respective branch of service.

The Armed Forces Service Award is awarded to all members of the armed forces who were on active duty on March 16, 1935 and thereafter. The awarding follows Hitler's directives that the 1st and 2nd Class shall be authorized of the commanders-in-chief of the three branches of the armed forces. Awarding of the 3rd Class shall be through the authorization of the divisional commanding general's commanding admirals or the commanding officers of the Luftwaffe.

The Service Award 4th Class shall be authorized through the unit level.

Civil Service Honor Award 1st Class (40 years service) golden

2nd Class (25 years service) silver

a) The Civil Service Honor Award

(Das Treudienst-Ehrenzeichen)

As the result of the introduction of the Service Awards for the Armed Forces Hitler established on January 30, 1938, the Civil Service Honor Award, the Police Service Award, SS Service Award and the National Work Program *(Reichsarbeitsdienst) Award.*

The Civil Service Honor Award given to civil servants, clerks and public service workers is a cross with a wreath of oakleaves between the arms. In the center of the obverse is a black enameled swastika. The reverse has the inscription "For Loyal Service" *(designed by Professor Richard Klein, Munich)* set in a square center. It is awarded in two levels: Silver for 25 years service and Golden for 40 years service. An appropriate miniature cross is worn on the ribbon bar.

With the awarding of the 1st level, the 2nd level will no longer be worn but will remain with the recipient. The Civil Service Honor Award can be worn together with the Armed Forces Service Award.

The request for the award goes through the Secretary of State for approval by Hitler. The award with the certificate is then made.

Civil Service Honor Award
Special Level

Police Service Award 3rd Level
(8 years Service)

For workers and other personnel employed in the free economic system, Hitler authorized a special level for the Civil Service Honor Award for 50 years continuous service to one employer. This Civil Service Honor Award is a silver cross with a golden wreath of oakleaves between the arms and a golden 50 on the obverse upper arm. On the reverse within the center square is the inscription "For Loyal Work." When worn on the ribbon bar, a miniature of the cross is attached. Requests for this award must go through administrative channels to the chancellery for approval.

c) The Police Service Award

(Die Polizeidienstauszeichnung)

The Police Service Award is authorized in three levels:

completion of 8 years service — silver medal
completion of 18 years service — silver cross
completion of 25 years service — golden cross

On the obverse of the medal and cross is the National Police Eagle. On the reverse of the medal is the number 8 and as on the crosses the inscription "For Loyal Service in the Police" *(designed by Professor Richard Klein, Munich)*. Woven into the ribbon of the 1st and 2nd level

Golden Police Service Cross 1st Level (25 years service)

2nd Level (18 years service) is silver

is the National Police Eagle. The 2nd level is embroidered in silver thread and gold thread for the 1st level.

When awarded the higher level, the lower level may not be worn but remains with the recipient. The Police Service Award may be worn adjacent to the Service Award of the Armed Forces.

The award request is routed through the SS Command Headquarters or the Chief of the German Police to the Secretary of State and to the Chancellery for approval.

d) The SS Service Award
(Die SS-dienstauszeichnung)

The SS-Service Award is given in recognition of loyal proficient service in the SS, SS-Reserves, SS-Death Heads Units and the SS-Junker Schools.

The SS-Service Award is authorized in four levels:

1. to non-commissioned officers and men after 4 years of proficient loyal service — the 4th level
2. to officers, non-commissioned officers and men after 8 years service — the 3rd level
3. to officers, non-commissioned officers and men after 12 years service — the 2nd level
4. to officers, non-commissioned officers and men after 25 years service — the 1st level

Includes service acquired during the organization of the NSDAP

Die SS-dienstauszeichnung 4th level (4years service)

Reverse

SS-Service Award

3rd level (8 years service)

2nd level (12 years service) silver

1st level (25 years service) golden

The SS-Service Award *(designed by Professor Karl Diebitsch, Munich)* 4th level is a round blackened medal. On the obverse are the Sig runes enclosed within a wreath of oakleaves. On the reverse is the number 4.

The SS-Service Award 3rd level is a round bronze medal. The obverse shows a swastika with *Sig* runes in the center surrounded by a wreath of oakleaves. The reverse shows the number 8.

The SS-Service Award 2nd level is a silver swastika with Sig runes in the center surrounded by a wreath of oakleaves.

The SS-Service Award 1st level is a golden swastika with Sig runes in the center surrounded by a wreath of oakleaves.

The reverse of all levels has the inscription "For Loyal Service in the SS."

The ribbon of the 1st and 2nd levels have embroidered Sig runes in the respective color of the award.

The SS-Service Award 1st and 2nd levels is the first decoration of the National State to use the swastika as a decoration or honor award and not just as the National Emblem.

When awarded the SS-Service Award in a higher level, the lower level can no longer be worn. The SS-Service Award can be worn along with the Service Award of the Armed Forces.

The award request is routed through the SS Command Headquarters or the Chief of the German Police to the Secretary of State and to the Chancellery for approval.

e) The Service Award of the National Work Program
(Die Dienstauszeichnung für den Reichsarbeitsdienst)

The National Work Program Service Award is an oval medal bordered by a wreath of oakleaves. In the obverse center is the symbol of the National Work Program showing a spade with a small swastika, point up, between the stylized ends of two wheat stalks. The reverse has the inscription "For Loyal Service in the National Work Program." The National Work Program Service Award is authorized in four levels:

4th level awarded on completion of 4 years service — bronze
3rd level awarded on completion of 12 years service — silver

The Service Award for the National Work Program

4th level (4 years service) *2nd level (18 years service)*

3rd level (12 years service) silver

1st level (25 years service) golden

Women's Service Award
2nd level (18 years service)

Customs-Border Security
Honor Award

2nd level awarded on completion of 18 years service —
silver with an embroidered silver National emblem
1st level awarded on completion of 25 years service —
golden with an embroidered golden National emblem

When awarded the higher level, the lower level may not be worn but remains with the recipient. The National Work Service Award may be worn next to the Armed Forces Service Award.

The Women's National Work Service Award shows on the obverse a large swastika between the stylized ends of two wheat stalks. The medal is worn suspended from a bow. The 1st and 2nd levels have a golden or a silver National eagle attached to the ribbon.

Requests for the awards are channeled through the National Work Program Headquarters to the Chancellery.

f) The Customs-Border Security Honor Award

(Das Zollgrenzschutz-Ehrenzeichen)

On February 17, 1939, Hitler authorized the Customs-Border Security Honor Award in recognition of loyal service in the Customs Service and the Border Security Service.

The Customs-Border Security Merit Cross can be awarded to:

1. Senior officials responsible for Customs and Border security after 4 years Border service,
2. Mid-management officials for Customs and Border security after
   a) 4 years of Border Security service,
   b) 8 years of civil administrative Border Security service.

The Customs-Border Security Honor Award is a bronze cross. In the obverse middle is an Acanthus leaves wreath open at the top surrounding the National Eagle. The reverse shows the inscription "For Loyal Service in Customs-Border Security." The cross is suspended from a corn flower blue ribbon and worn on the left breast. The ribbon has an embroidered National Eagle surrounded by an Acanthus leaves wreath open at the top.

The Customs-Border Security Merit Cross may be worn adjacent to the Service Awards of the Armed Forces.

5. Air Safety Honor Award

(Das Luftschutz-Ehrenzeichen)

As ordered by Hitler, the Air Safety Honor Award was established on January 30, 1938, in two classes. The second class is given to per-

Air Raid Protection Award

2nd class

1st cross

sonnel in Germany who were active in the service of the Air Safety programs after January 30, 1933, and who have earned special recognition for meritorious service. The 1st Class is awarded to personnel who have distinguished themselves in the Air Safety program.

The award of the 1st Class did not require the recipient to have the 2nd Class.

Both Classes are totally different. The 2nd Class is a darkish gray circular oxidized medal having an oakleaves wreath border. In the obverse center is a swastika surrounded by the inscription "For Merit in Air Safety." The 1st Class is a golden cross with wide edged arms. In the obverse center of the cross is a raised swastika. A circular border containing the same inscription as on the 2nd Class is placed on the arms and surrounding the swastika. The reverse of both awards has the year "1938" *(designed by graphics designer Egon Jantke, Berlin).*

The ribbon for both Classes is a light lavender with a black-white-red edge. The 2nd Class cannot be worn by a recipient who receives the 1st Class. The request for these awards must go through the State Minister of Air Safety and Air Control to the Chancellery.

6. The Fire Service Merit Award

(Das Feuerwehr-Ehrenzeichen)

The State Interior Ministry on December 22, 1936, by the authorization of paragraph 11 of the regulations of November 14, 1935, created a State Fire Service Merit Award to be only awarded by the Interior Ministry. By the revision of January 30, 1938, the award would be authorized only by Hitler.

The regulations of the two Classes will be maintained. The 2nd level or Class remains unchanged: a silver framed white enamel cross with red flames in the arms. Between each arm surrounding the medallion is the inscription "For Merit in the Fire Service." The 1st Class, a larger version, has been modified to be worn suspended from a ribbon and can be worn with a group. The 1st Class has a gold frame and gold inscription whereas the 2nd class is silver.

The ribbon for both classes is red-white-red.

The 1st Class is awarded to members of the professional fire brigades (Fire Protection Police) or volunteer fire units or other individuals displaying special achievements with the Fire Services or for outstanding conduct during fire control.

The 2nd Class is awarded to members of the professional fire brigades (Fire Protection Police) or other volunteer fire units after May

Fire Service Merit Cross 1st Class

2nd Class is silver

Mining Merit Medal

1, 1936 in recognition of 25 years loyal and honorable service.

With the award of the 1st Class the recipient will no longer wear the 2nd Class.

The Fire Service Honor Award can also be awarded to foreigners. Recommendations will be sent to the Chief of the SS, Chief of the German Police and the State Chancellery Chief of Personnel .

7. The Mining Service Merit Award

(Das Grubenwehr-Ehrenzeichen)

The State Ministry of Economics by the authorization of paragraph 12 of the regulations of November 14, 1935, regarding Titles, Orders and Decorations from May 15, 1934 on November 13, 1936 created a State Mining Merit Honor Award. By the revision of January 30, 1938, the mining award would be authorized only by Hitler. It is a silver medal having on the obverse the State Eagle emblem on a crossed hammer and iron pick and on the reverse the inscription "For Merit in the Mining Service." It is suspended from an orange ribbon with black side stripes and white edges. It can also be worn with a group.

The Mining Service Merit Medal is awarded to:

1. members of the mining service completing 15 years of accident-free service.
2. members of the mining service with shorter service but unable to work any longer in the mines as a result of an accident.
3. members of the mining service or other miners in recognition of special service or distinguished service during a mine rescue.

Recommendations will be directed to the State Ministry of Economics and the State Chancellery Chief of Personnel.

8. The Life Saving - Rescue Medal

(Die Rettungsmedaille)

The Life Saving Medal is suspended from a ribbon and is patterned after the 1833 Prussian Life Saving Medal. It is a silver medal having on the obverse an eagle with a swastika on its chest. On the reverse is the inscription "Für Rettung aus Gefahr" *(For Rescue from Danger)*. It is suspended from an orange ribbon with white edges.

The regulations adopted by Hitler defining the rescue requirements were authorized on July 10, 1937. The Life Saving Medal on the Ribbon was awarded when the rescuers life was placed in extreme dan-

Life Saving - Rescue Medal

ger. If the rescue was somewhat less dangerous for the rescuer, then the Life Saving Rescue Commemorative Medal would be given. This is a non-portable silver medal measuring 50 cm. in diameter. The requirements for this medal are somewhat less stringent than for the Life Saving Rescue Medal on the Ribbon. For a life saving rescue without risk of loss of one's life, the rescuer will receive public praise and in some cases a monetary reward will be given. A young rescuer under 18 years shall receive the Life Saving Rescue Medal on the Ribbon when reaching the age of 18. They will receive the medal in the name of Hitler through the civil administration authorities. However, the Life Saving Rescue Commemorative Medal will be given regardless of age.

Requests will be sent directly to the civil authorities in the county where the recipient lives and then forwarded to the Chancellery. Requests for the medal for soldiers and military civil administrators will be directed to the Armed Forces High Command. Further, requests shall be directed to the Chief of Staff of the SA, the Chief of the SS, the Chief of the NSKK, the Chief of the NSFK and Chief of the State Labor Service who shall have the awarding authority for members of their respective organizations. Requests for foreigners shall be directed to the Ministry of Foreign Affairs.

9. The Colonial Badge

(Das Kolonialabzeichen)

The Colonial Badge was authorized on April 18, 1922 by the Ministry of Reconstruction. The badge is silver gray and shows on the obverse an elephant and the inscription "Südsee ★ Afrika ★ Kiautschou" *(South Seas - Africa - Kiaochow)*. It is worn without a ribbon on the left breast.

The Colonial Badge

The badge was awarded on request to Colonial Germans who served in the interests and service of the former German Protectorates during the World War.

The Colonial Badge was first awarded through the Ministry of Reconstruction until December 31, 1935. Now the authority for the awarding of the Colonial Badge was given to the Foreign Affairs Office. It still had to be requested. Since January 1, 1936, the Colonial Badge was personally awarded by Hitler.

Since 1922 approximately 8500 Colonial Badges have been awarded. Now that there is no longer requests for the badge, the issuance has ended. The recipient receives a document with the signature of Hitler. Requests for the award are directed to the Foreign Affairs Office of the Chancellery.

10. The March 13, 1938 Commemorative Medal

(Die Medaille zur Erinnerung an den 13. März 1938)

On the historic day of the return of Austria to the Third Reich, Hitler authorized on May 1, 1938, the "March 13, 1938 Commemorative Medal" for meritorious service during the uniting of Austria and Germany.

The obverse of the silver medal shows the symbolic return of Austria as part of the National Socialist Greater Germany. The medal is a smaller version of the 1938 Party Day badge *(designed by Professor Richard Klein of Munich)*. The reverse shows the date 13. März 1938 and the inscription "Ein Volk, ein Reich, ein Führer" *(One People, one State, one Leader)*. The ribbon is red with black-white-black edge stripes.

The medal is awarded to persons in Austria or the old national areas who were involved in the unification.

The March 13, 1938 Commemorative Medal

Special recognition is given to the members of the NSDAP in Austria, persons who in the battle for unification lost their homes or were incarcerated or forced to leave the country, or are widows and parents of those who gave their lives in the effort of unification. The medal is also awarded to members of the armed forces, the police, the SS, the NSKK and the NSFK who took part in the unification as well as officials and all public service personnel involved in the unification.

The award of this medal has been stopped on December 31, 1940. A total of 318,689 medals have been awarded.

11. The October 1, 1938 Commemorative Medal

(Die Medaille zur Erinnerung an den 1 Oktober 1938)

The time for the Sudetenland German area to return to the German homeland had come. Hitler authorized on October 18, 1938 the "October 1, 1938 Commemorative Medal" for meritorious service in the reuniting of the Sudetenland German area with the Greater Germany. The medal is bronze and the obverse is the same as the "March 13, 1938 Commemorative Medal." The reverse shows the date "1. Oktober 1938."

The October 1, 1938 Commemorative Medal with the Ribbon Clasp

The ribbon is black-red-black having white edges.

The award follows the same regulations for qualification as the "March 13, 1938 Commemorative Medal."

The regulations were amended by Hitler on May 1, 1939 that the "October 1, 1938 Commemorative Medal" will also be awarded for meritorious service in the creation of the Protectorate of Bohemia and Moravia.

Those individuals who have already received this medal and involved in the creation of the Protectorate of Bohemia and Moravia shall recieve a bronze clasp to be attached to the suspension ribbon. The clasp shows, in relief, the Prague Castle *(designed by sculpter Hanish-Conée, Berlin)*.

The awarding of this medal and clasp ended on December 31, 1940. A total of 1,162,617 medals and 134,563 clasps have been awarded.

12. The Return of Memel Commemorative Medal

(Die Medaille zur Erinnerung an die Heimkehr des Memellandes)

To commemorate the return of the Memel area to Germany, Hitler authorized the "Return of Memel Commemorative Medal" on May 1, 1939. It is awarded for meritorious service in the return of the Memel area to Germany.

The medal is dark bronze and the obverse is the same as the previously described medals. The reverse has the inscription "Zur Erinnerung an die Heimkehr des Memellandes 22. März 1939" *(To Commemorate the Return of the Memel area on March 22, 1939)*. The medal is worn suspended from a green-white-red *(the colors of Memel)* on the left breast.

The awarding of this medal ended on December 31, 1940. A total of 31,322 medals have been awarded.

The Return of Memel Commemorative Medal

Reverse

13. The Honor Cross of the German Mother

(Das Ehrenkreuz der Deutschen Mutter)

In recognition and thanks to the German mother, often referred to in his speeches, Hitler established on December 16, 1938 the "Honor Cross of the German Mother."

The Honor Cross is awarded in three Classes:

The third Class to mothers with four or five children.

The second Class to mothers with six or seven children.

The first Class to mothers with eight or more children.

The Honor Cross has widening arms and an elongated bottom arm. The arms are blue enameled with a white enameled edge. In the center is a separately attached white enameled medallion with a black swastika. Surrounding the center is the inscription "Der Deutschen Mutter" *(The German Mother)*. Between the arms are metal rays *(designed by Dipl.-Ing. Architect Franz Berberich, Munich)*.

The reverse has the date "16. Dezember 1938" and the facsimile signature of Hitler.

The metal parts are in the third Class bronze, in the second Class silver and in the first Class golden.

The Honor Cross ribbon is blue and white striped narrow ribbon worn at the neck.

The criteria for the award is:

1. The parents and children are of German blood,
2. The mother is worthy,
3. The children are born alive.

Requests for receiving the Honor Cross of the German Moth-

Honor Cross of the German Mother 1st Class

2nd Class in silver
3rd Class in bronze

ers are directed through the Office of the local Mayor or by request of the local NSDAP official and approval of the area State office of Childrens Welfare. The request is then sent to other civil administrators for proper action. After receiving approval from the Health Departmant all the information is collected by the local NSDAP official and forwarded to proper officials in the Ministry authorizing this award in the Chancellery. After official approval, the Honor Cross of the German Mother will be awarded with a recognition ceremony on Mothers Day or by the local area NSDAP official. The award is presented with a document signed by Hitler and the Secretary of State. In the event the Honor Cross for the German Mother is denied the mother, there will be no recognition.

14. The Honor Award for German Civil Welfare

(Das Ehrenzeichen für deutsche Volkspflege)

On May 1, 1939, Hitler authorized the establishment of the "Honor Award for German Civil Welfare" to recognize meritorious service in welfare, the Winter Help programs, the care of the sick and wounded in peace and wartime, the life saving service and also care of fellow German countrymen in a foreign country. Also in the new regulations, Hitler no longer allowed the President of the German Red Cross to award the Red Cross Honor Cross and Medal.

The Honor Award for German Civil Welfare will replace the Red Cross Honor Cross and Medal. The current purpose of the new award provides a wider scope. The Red Cross Honor awards will be presented only for meritorious service in the German Red Cross. The newly established Honor Award for German Civil Welfare encompasses a wider range of award criteria, and is elevated to a State honor, and is awarded by Hitler.

The Honor Award is awarded in four Classes:

1. The Honor Cross for German Welfare 1st Class
2. The Honor Cross for German Welfare 2nd Class
3. The Honor Cross for German Welfare 3rd Class
4. The Honor Medal for German Welfare.

Hitler reserves the right to award, for extraordinary recognition, a special Class of The Honor Cross for German Welfare 1st Class with Star.

Through the amendment of January 30, 1942, Hitler authorized the Honor Cross and Medal to be awarded with swords and swords on the ribbon for wartime distinguished conduct and personal bravery. The award criteria will be set by the Commander-in-Chief of the Armed Forces and the State Minister of the Chancellery. However, the award of swords will be only allowed for the Honor Cross 3rd Class and Honor Medal. Since the 2nd Class is without a ribbon and the 1st Class is worn suspended from the neck, no swords will attached or added to the original form of the Honor Award.

Honor Cross for German Welfare
2nd Class

Until further notice these awards will be given only to male and female personnel (no armed forces personnel) serving in the combat zone in the Eastern theater of war.

In this new form the Honor Cross and Honor Medal resembles the former honor awards of the German Red Cross. However, the old Red Cross eagle has been replaced with the newly designed national eagle on the obverse of the cross and medal. *(Designed by Prof. Richard Klein, Munich).*

Honor Cross for German Welfare
3rd Class

Honor Medal for German Welfare

Requests for award authorization must be directed to the Chiefs of the NSDAP Chancellery, Ministry of the Interior, Ministry of Works Administration, Ministry of Propaganda, Ministry of Foreign Affairs and the Commander-in-Chief of the Armed Forces. The latter only for the award with swords on the ribbon — and the President of the German Red Cross.

When receiving the higher Class of the award, the lower Classes will not be worn. When receiving the Honor Award of the German Welfare, the previously awarded German Red Cross awards will not be worn.

15. The German Westwall Honor Medal

(Das Deutsche Schutzwall-Ehrenzeichen)

On August 2, 1939, Hitler authorized as a recognition of thanks for meritorious service in the design and building of the protective fortifications in western Germany, the "German Westwall Honor Medal." It has been awarded to personnel who worked on the construction of the fortifications thus providing safety for the German nation.

German Westwall Honor Medal

The German Westwall Honor Medal is a bronze oval medal. On the obverse is a bunker with crossed sword and shovel above but below the National Eagle Emblem. The reverse has the inscription "Für Arbeit zum Schutze Deutschlands" *(For Work for the Protection of Germany)* *(designed by Prof. R. Klein, Munich).*

The German Westwall Honor Medal is suspended from a brown ribbon with white stripes and a brown edge and worn on the left breast.

The request and award of the German Westwall Honor Medal will be directed to the Commander-in-Chief of the Armed Forces, the Inspector General of German Roadways and the Chief of the State Works Program.

The request is forwarded assuming all guidelines have been met, to Hitler through the Secretary of State and Chief of Personnel of the Chancellery. Persons who have received the October 1, 1938 Commemorative Medal or the Return of Memel Commemorative Medal shall not receive the German Westwall Honor Medal.

The German Westwall Honor Medal remains with the family upon the death of the recipient as a remembrence.

Since January 31, 1941 awards of the medal has stopped. A total of 622064 Honor Medals have been awarded.

16 Non-Wearable State Decorations

(Nicht tragbare staatliche Auszeichnungen)

Next to wearable decorations and honor awards, except for the previously described Life Saving Rescue Commemorative Medal, Hitler established the Eagle Medallion of the German State and the Goethe Medal for Art and Science.

The Eagle Medallion of the German State is a round bronze medallion set into a bronze base. The obverse has the National German Eagle while the reverse shows the recipients name engraved.

This seldom-awarded Eagle Medallion is given in recognition of outstanding creative contributions to the German people by persons of a high academic background. Until January 1, 1943 a total of only 60 Eagle Medallions of the German State had been awarded.

The Goethe Medal for Art and Science is a matt silvered medal. The obverse shows the head of Goethe and on the reverse is the National German Eagle above the inscription "Für Kunst und Wissenschaft" *(For Art and Science)*. Around the edge is the inscription "Gestiftet vom Reichspräsidenten von Hindenburg 1932" *(Established by President von Hindenburg 1932) (Designed by Sculptor Hanisch-Concée, Berlin)*.

The Goethe Medal was established on the 100th anniversary of the death of Goethe in the year 1932 by the late President von Hindenburg. It was awarded in recognition of outstanding merit by distinguished individuals at the Goethe festivals in and outside of Germay. Going beyond the original intent, the Goethe Medal is awarded for outstanding achievements in art and science. Until January 1, 1943 a total of 467 medals have been awarded.

Requests and recommendations for the award of the Eagle Medallion and the Goethe Medal will be submitted through the offices of the Minister and President of the Chancellery for final determination by Hitler.

(Reduced, the medallion measures 11 cm.)

Goethe Medal for Art and Science

Obverse

Reverse

II. The Orders and Awards of the National Socialist Movement

1. The Honor Badge for Members under 100,000 Golden Party Badge

(Goldenes Parteiabzeichen)

Through a decree in October, 1933, Hitler authorized that a special award be given to all Party members who had, as of November 9, 1933, registered numbers from 1 to 100,000 and who had unbroken Party membership. It will be called the Golden Party Badge.

The Golden Party Badge will have a golden wreath surrounding the party badge. The reverse of the badge will have the issue number of the member engraved.

Golden Party Badge

The Treasury will establish guidelines to ensure that requirements are met in order to receive the badge. It can be requested by and/or given to those members who joined after the founding of the NSDAP on February 27, 1925 and who have the issue number between 1 and 100,000. The Treasury Department will make the presentations. The member certificate shall be hand-written. Hitler reserves the right to award the Golden Party Badge for special recognition.

The Golden Party Badge is worn in two sizes: the large Golden Party Badge will be worn on the service uniform, the small badge will be worn on the suit jacket *(refer to wearing instructions)*.

In the event of the death of the member, the Golden Party Badge will remain with the family. Because of the numbered certificate, no one will wear the badge of the deceased. The right to wear the Golden Party Badge ceases when the member leaves the NSDAP.

2. The Blood Order Medal

(Der Blutorden)

During March of 1934, Hitler authorized the "Honor Medal of November 9, 1923" also called the "Blood Order" to commemorate the November 9, 1923 uprising of the National Socialist movement.

Obverse

Reverse

The Blood Order Medal is silver and four centimeters in diameter. The obverse shows an eagle with outspread wings grasping an oakleaf wreath. Inside the wreath is the date "9. Nov." to the right is the inscription "München 1923-1933" *(Munich 1923-1933)*. The reverse shows the entrance of the Feldherrnhalle in relief, and directly above is the angled swastika with sun rays in the background. Along the top edge is the inscription "UND IHR HABT DOCH GESIEGT" *(and we have won after all)*. Every medal has the incised party number of the recipient on the reverse. The ribbon is red with a black and white edge. The Blood Order Medal will be worn in the buttonhole of the right breast pocket of the brown shirt or the service jacket. In the armed forces it will be worn on the tunic in the right breast pocket buttonhole. On the dress tunic it will be worn from the second buttonhole.

The Blood Order Medal is awarded by Hitler. The bestowal follows the regulations established by decree for the active participation on November 23, 1923. After the reuniting of Austria with Germany, Hitler amended the awarding regulation to include May 30, 1938 in recognition of special merit in the battle to unify Germany.

Awarding criteria for the Blood Order Medal:

1. For active participation on November 9,1923
   a) To members of the SA, War Flag Association, or the Oberland Society, and those engaged in the resistance in Munich.

   b) To members of the armed forces or the police who were members of the SA on November 9, 1923, the War Flag Association, or the Oberland Society who were unable to participate at the Munich resistance but openly supported the movement which resulted in their losing their employment. This will include members of the armed forces or police who, due to their political beliefs, voluntarily left the national army or police. Included are members of the Munich Infantry School who actively took part in the activities on November 9, 1923.

   c) To members of the SA, War Flag Association or the Oberland Society, who on November 9, 1923 were not allowed to participate in the resistance because of police interference.

2. For those party members of old Germany and the Ostmark *(Austria)* who for their political belief were:
   a) sentenced to death but later commuted to life imprisonment,
   b) sentenced to prison (also in Austria) for a minimum of at least one year,
   c) or severely wounded.

It is understood that one must be a member of the Party before the award can be made. To qualify under number1above, membership in the Party, SA or SS must have been prior to January 1, 1932, with uninterrupted service to the Party, the SA, the SS or the NSKK.

The medal is not subject to any legal claims.

Requests for the medal by either the member or a prominent person must be approved by five party members appointed by the Order Commission of the National Treasury who have received the Blood Order Medal and the Golden Party Badge. The recipient will receive from the National Treasury a document authorized and signed by Hitler and the National Treasurer.

The right to wear the Blood Order Medal ceases:

1. by separation from the Party,
2. by personnel holding an official position in the Party and being declared unqualified,
3. by order of a court decision of the Orders Commission.

In such cases the Blood Order Medal, ribbon, award document and membership certificate will be returned through proper channels to the Orders Commission.

Upon the death of the Recipient the Blood Order Medal will remain with the family.

3. The Coburg Badge

(Das Coburger Abzeichen)

The Coburg Badge was authorized by Hitler on October 14, 1932 in commemoration of the 10th anniversary of the October 14-15, 1922 German Day in Coburg. Through the leadership of Hitler, with 800 members of the SA from Munich and other Bavarian cities, the Red Terror was broken in Coburg. The right to wear the special Coburg badge was authorized on November 6, 1936 through the SA headquarters. The wearing of the badge can be withdrawn by Hitler or the Leader of the Party Chancellery.

4. The Nuremberg Party Badge of 1929

(Das Nürnberger Parteiabzeichen von 1929)

As a special honor badge, the Party through regulations of November 6, 1936, established the Nuremberg Party Badge for the 4th National Party Day of the NSDAP in Nuremberg on August 1-4, 1929.

Coburg Badge

Nuremberg Badge

Braunschweig Badge

Permission to wear the Nurnberg Party Badge is granted by the senior district leader. The wearing of the badge can be withdrawn by Hitler or the Leader of the Party Chancellery.

5. The Badge of the SA Assembly in Braunschweig 1931

(Das Abzeichen vom SA-Treffen in Braunschweig 1931)

Through the regulations of November 6, 1936, a special Party Honor Badge commemorating the SA Assembly in Braunschweig on October 17-18, 1931 was created. On this date 104,000 SA and SS participated in a six hour march in review before Hitler and the first inspection of the SA Motor and the NSKK units.

The permission to wear the Braunschweig Badge must be confirmed by the Senior SA Party leader or above. The wearing of the badge can be revoked by the Chief-of-Staff of the SA.

6. Traditional District Badges

(Die Traditions-Gauabzeichen)

The Traditional District Badges may be worn with Hitler's approval, as follows:

1

1. The combined badge for districts of Saxony, Bavarian Austria, Halle-Merseburg, Hesse-Nassau, Magdeburg-Anhalt, Mecklenburg, Lübeck.
2. Badge for Berlin 1926,
3. Badge for Baden,
4. Badge for Thüringen,
5. Badge for East Hannover,
6. Badge for Danzig,
7. Badge for East Prussia,
8. Badge for Essen.

Permission to wear the District Badges is granted by the senior district leader. The wearing of the badges can be revoked by Hitler or the NSDAP Leader.

2

3

Approximately 30 awards in gold were awarded

4

5

7. The Golden Hitler Youth Badge

(Das Goldene Hitler-Jugend-Abzeichen)

With permission from Hitler on June 23, 1934 the Golden Hitler Youth Badge was established as an honor award to the National Youth Leader in recognition of leadership and long service or other special achievements in the Hitler Youth organization. This form is a golden

6

7

framed rhomboid having in the center a golden square field with a black swastika in a red and white field.

Awarding of the Hitler Youth Badge until July 31, 1937 to the Youth boy and girl associations which began with the first awarding on October 2, 1937 (first National Youth Day in Potsdam) to members of the Hitler Youth and the German Young People *(Jungvolks)*, NSS, BdM in the HJ. Having unbroken membership in the Hitler Youth and in the transfer to the NSDAP, the Hitler Youth Badge may be worn on the uniform. This allows immedeate recognition. Also members of the National Work Service and the armed forces will also be allowed to wear the badge.
The right to wear the Golden Hitler Youth Badge is allowed when the recipient leaves the NSDAP and no longer wears the uniform. The Leader of the National Hitler Youth can grant the right for the recipient to wear the badge indefinitely as a sign of achievement recognition.

8

Awarded in Gold under extraordinary circumstances

Golden Hitler Youth Badge
(With Oakleaves at right)

The Golden Hitler Youth Honor Badge with the Golden Oakleaves border is awarded by the National Youth Leader for meritorious service in the Hitler Youth.

8. The Service Awards of the NSDAP
(Die Dienstauszeichnung der NSDAP)

Hitler authorized the Service Awards of theNSDAP on April 2, 1939.

The Service Award of the NSDAP established by Hitler were for all members of the Party from the highest to the lowest. It was worn on the uniform or when active in special units or when holding an honorary appointment to recognize loyal service to the Party.

The Service Award is a cross with slightly curved arms. In the center of the cross is the National Eagle with an oakleaves wreath. Between the arms are rays.

The Service Awards are in three Classes, for 10, 15 and 25 years active service in the NSDAP.

The Service Award for 10 years service is in bronze and suspended from a 3 cm. wide dark brown ribbon with two narrow white side stripes. The Service Award for 15 years service is silver with the arms having dark blue enamel. The ribbon is blue with two narrow silver side stripes. The Service Award for 25 years service is gold with the arms having white enamel. The ribbon is red.

NSDAP Service Award
for 10 years service

NSDAP Service Award for 15 years service

NSDAP Service Award for 25 years service

The edge stripes are white having a small gold center stripe.

The Service Awards of the NSDAP may be worn on a mounted group. Women recipients shall wear the Service Award suspended from a 15 mm. wide ribbon around the neck. On the small ribbon bar the ribbon will have a small National Eagle within a wreath on the proper color of the specific Class.

The award can be given in special circumstances for distinguished service by some members or to those members in a Party association upon the recommendation of the administrative personnel of the NSDAP. The three Classes of the Service Awards of the NSDAP may be worn consecutively on the mounted group or on the ribbon bar. Upon the award of the higher Class, the recipient is permitted to wear the lower Class.

9. The "Work Pioneer" Honor Badge

(Das Ehrenzeichen „Pionier der Arbeit")

During August of 1940, Hitler established the Honor Badge for the "Work Pioneer" to be awarded on the recommendation the Chief of the National Organization of the NSDAP and the Leaders of the German

Works Program and awarded by Hitler personally. In the words of the Leader of the National Organization, Pg. Dr. Ley, this award is the highest of the achievements program, and will be an inspiration for those competing by increasing the desire to receive the highest honor award. This award is the highest in the works area of the National Socialist State. It is to be awarded to countrymen working in a "National Socialist Model Factory" having the most outstanding participation in the exemplary conduct of management and thereby achieving the recognition of receiving the Golden Flag.

Honor Award "Work Pioneer"

The Honor Award is an oval badge having a golden laurel leaf wreath edge. On a red enameled background is a golden German Workers Front cogged wheel emblem having a white enameled background on which is a black swastika. Above the wheel is a golden National Eagle. The badge is worn on the left breast.

With the document dated August 7, 1940, Hitler awarded the Honor Badge to the management leader of the Friedrich Krupp Joint Stock Company in Essen, Krupp von Bohlen und Halbach. The management received the "National Socialist Model Factory" award on May 1, 1940.

Others receiving the award
on May 1, 1941
National Minister Max Amann,
National Post Minister Dr. Wilhelm Ohnesorge,
Professor Dipl. Engineer Willy Messerschmitt,
on September 23, 1941
Dr. Engineer e.h. Robert Bosch,
on May 1, 1942
Professor Dr. Engineer e.h., Dr. Phil. h.c. Ernst Heinkel,
Professor Dr. Engineer h.c. Ferdinand Porsche
National Economics Minister and National Bank President
Walther Funk.

III. Badges

(Abzeichen)

Orders and decorations as before stated, usually are awarded by Hitler. Along with orders and decorations are awards having various Classes and badges which are awarded in recognition of personal distinctions and achievements. In the highest catagory are the military awards of the armed forces.

Not included in this book are the many other types of badges which do not have the characteristics of achievement badges, such as the uniform badges which are awarded in recognition of military accomplishment or performance. Examples are the matt gray embroidered proficiency badges worn on the lower left arm of the Airman's blouse or tunic, or the embroidered proficiency badge for anti-aircraft defense. Also not included in this section are the badges of members of the NSDAP, recognition for contributions, Winter Help Works, or the German Red Cross, badges for members of congress, commercial firms or long time employees and so on.

A. Military Badges of the Armed Forces

(Die Waffenabzeichen der Wehrmacht)

Through paragraph 1 of the regulations of May 3, 1942 regarding the protection of the military badges of the armed forces, Hitler decreed that:

Military Badge of the Armed Forces are protected:

1. on the occasion of an award for military distinction during this war.
2. by the award, through the High Command of the specific military branch of the recipient, in recognition of distinction or bravery.

The regulations also point out the punishment for the unauthorized wearing of the orders and awards. Specifically these protective regulations will be found in paragraph 6, section 1, letter b. established on July 1, 1937.

The Chief of the Armed Forces will determine which military awards of the armed forces will be protected under these regulations.

Military distinction badges will be the same for all members of the armed forces; however, there will be exceptions, such as the Narvik shield or special badges of certain branches of the armed forces.

The distinction and bravery badges of the army and Luftwaffe will be special for those branches of the armed forces.

Regulations regarding the protection of military badges of the armed forces of 3. May 1942, RGBl. I, p. 277; General Army Directive 1942, Publication 21, p. 408, No. 773; 1942, Publication 25 p. 498, No. 921. — Naval Regulation Directive 1942, Publication 29, p. 803, No. 695; 1942, Publication 36, p. 1000, No. 901. — Air Force Directive 1942, Publication 21, p. 767, No. 1272; 1942, Publication 35, p. 173, No. 2149; 1942, Publication 48, p. 1655, No. 2846.

I. Military Badges
a) Armed Forces

1. The Narvik Shield
(Der Narvikschild)

The Narvik shield was authorized on August 19, 1940, by Hitler and the Supreme Command of the Armed Forces to commemorate the successful heroic military engagement at Narvik through the outstanding cooperation of the army, navy and Luftwaffe.

Narvik shield

The shield was only to be worn on the left upper arm of the uniform. The army shield is silver color on field-gray cloth, for the navy the shield is golden on dark blue cloth and the Luftwaffe shield is silver on gray-blue cloth.

It is awarded to all participants in the landing at Narvik or with the Group Narvik. Also it is awarded to those killed in action. The awarding was by order of Hitler through the commander of the Group Narvik, Lt. General Dietl.

The recipient receives an award document. For the killed-in-action or those that have died from their wounds, the shield and document will go to the next-of-kin.

The Narvik shield can also be worn on the Party uniforms and state uniforms. On civilian clothes a miniature of the Narvik shield may be worn on the left coat lapel.

Regulations regarding the establishment of the Narvik Shield on 19. August 1940, RGBl. I, p. 1177, by specific orders: General Army Directive 1940, Part A, Publication 57, Section 11, p. 59, No. 59; 1941, Part A, Publication 19, Section 4, p. 17, No. 12. — Air Force Directive 1940, No. 46, p. 1321, — Naval Regulation Directive 1940, Publication 36, p. 738, No. 674; 1941, Publication 4, p. 46, No. 60.

2. The Cholm Shield

(Der Cholmschild)

To commemorate the heroic defense of Cholm against an overwhelming and numerically superior enemy Hitler established on July 1, 1942 the Cholm shield.

Cholm Shield

The Cholm shield was awarded to all military and attached personnel who served in the defense of Cholm between January 21 until May 5, 1942. Also included are those who participated in the evacuations by sea and air. Awarding of the shield was given to Major General Scherer, commander of Cholm. The recipients received a document. The shield was given beginning on 31 December 1942 and closed on April 1, 1943. For the killed-in-action or those that have died from their wounds, the shield and document will go to the next-of-kin.

The Cholm shield was to be worn on the left upper arm of the uniform. The shield can also be worn on the Party uniforms and state uniforms. On civilian clothes a miniature of the Cholm shield may be worn on the left coat lapel.

Regulations regarding the establishment of the Cholm Shield on 1 July 1942, RGBl. I, p. 455, by specific orders: General Army Directive 1942, Publication18, p. 319, No. 625; — Air Force Directive 1942, Publication 30, p. 1019, No. 1855 — Naval Regulation Directive 1942, Publication 29, p. 738, No. 805, No. 696.

3. The Crimea Shield

(Der Krimschild)

To commemorate the heroic campaign in the Crimea, Hitler established on July 25, 1942 the Crimea Shield.

Crimea shield

The Crimea shield is awarded as a combat badge to all armed forces personnel and persons attached to the armed forces who were in combat between September 21, 1941 until July 4, 1942 in the Crimea and south of Perekop, on land, air and sea and have complied with the following criteria:

a) engaged in combat,
b) wounded,
c) three months uninterrupted service in the Crimea.

The shield is awarded in the name of Hitler through General Field Marshal von Manstein. The recipient receives an award document. The award can be made posthumously. In this case the Crimea shield and document will be given the next-of-kin. The shield is worn on the left upper arm of the tunic. The Crimea shield can also be worn on the Party uniforms and state uniforms. On civilian clothes a miniature of the Crimea shield may be worn on the left coat lapel.

Regulations regarding the establishment of the Crimea Shield on 25 July 1942, RGBl. I, p. 487, by specific orders: General Army Directive 1942, Publication 20, p. 383, No. 717. — Air Force Directive 1942, Publication 33, p. 1115, No. 2029 — Naval Regulation Directive 1942, Publication 31, p. 862, No. 741.

4. The Bravery and Merit Award for Soldiers of the Eastern Nations

(Die Tapferkeits- und Verdienst-Auszeichnung für Angehörige der Ostvölker)

As a sign of recognition for bravery and merit, Hitler established on July 14, 1942, the Bravery and Merit Award for Soldiers of the Eastern Nations.

The award is given as a combat decoration with swords (bravery award) and as a merit decoration without swords (merit award) in the following Classes:

Bravery and Merit Award for Soldiers of the Eastern Nations

1st Class in Gold with Swords

1st Class in Silver without Swords

2nd Class in Bronze on dark green ribbon,
2nd Class in Silver on green with white side stripes,
2nd Class in Gold on light green with red side stripes,
1st Class in Silver
1st Class in Gold

Each Class of the 2nd Class can be awarded three times. To receive the higher Class, according to the regulations, the three lower Classes must have been received. The award of the 1st Class is predicated upon having received the highest 2nd Class. Through an outstanding display of bravery or distinguished meritorious service, the award of the higher Class can be made.

The award with swords will be given only for bravery by soldiers of the Eastern Nations when in combat under German orders. The award without swords will be given for meritorious service in the occupied Eastern areas by soldiers of the Eastern Nations.

With the award of the 1st Class in gold or silver a monetary gift can also be given.

2nd Class in Gold with Swords

2nd Class in Silver without Swords

The Bravery Award for Soldiers of the Eastern Nations can also be awarded to German soldiers as recognition of their leadership while either commanding or as members of a unit of the Eastern Nations. In order to qualify it is necessary to have received the 1939 2nd or 1st Class Iron Cross, or the 1939 Clasp to the 1st or 2nd Class 1914 Iron Cross or to receive both decorations at the same time. The awards in either Class can only be awarded once in the following manner:

2nd Class in Silver in combination with the 1939 2nd Class Iron Cross or the 1939 Clasp to the 1914 2nd Class Iron Cross,

1st Class in Silver in combination with the 1939 1st Class Iron Cross or the 1939 Clasp to the 1914 1st Class Iron Cross.

2nd Class in Bronze with Swords

The award of the Merit Decoration for Soldiers of the Eastern Nations to Germans (specifically to German administrators in the Eastern occupied areas) is not foreseen.

Authorization to award the decoration with swords will be through commanders of the German armed forces with the rank of Division Commander. Troops engaged in anti-partisan activities will be awarded the decoration through the Police Chief in the areas involved holding the rank of a division commander. The decoration without swords will be authorized by the Minister of the occupied Eastern areas. The recipients will receive an award document.

The 2nd Class will be worn suspended from the second buttonhole or from a mounted group. The 1st Class is a pinback and worn on the left breast.

Regulations regarding the establishment of the "Bravery and Merit Award for Soldiers of the Eastern Nations" on 14 July 1942, RGBl. I, p. 463, by specific orders: General Army Directive 1942, Publication 19, p. 339, No. 667. — Air Force Directive 1942, Publication 32, p. 1082, No. 1963 — Naval Regulation Directive 1942, Publication 31, p. 860, No. 740.

b) Army

1. The Infantry Combat Badge

(Das Infanterie-Sturmabzeichen)

The Infantry Combat Badge was established on December 20, 1939 as a recognition of combat action as an infantryman. Awarded by the Army commander-in-chief upon the recommendation of the infantry company commander.

The Infantry Combat Badge in silver will be awarded to officers, NCO's and enlisted men of rifle companies not in Motorized Infantry Divisions, and to Mountain Troop companies who from January 1, 1940 completed the following:

Infantry Combat Badge

In Bronze for Motorized Infantry Regiments

1. combat in three assaults,
2. in the front lines,
3. armed with hand weapons during assault.
4. on three different combat days.

the badge is awarded for counter-assaults, assaults of particular importance, patrols and patroling activities resulting in combat, and hand-to-hand combat. Criteria also includes the soldier or individual personally and single-handedly destroying an enemy tank.

All of the above can be placed into the Classification as number 5 and the Infantry Com bat Badge can be given as a special award under the qualification as in number 1 above.

Through Army General Order of June 1, 1940, the awarding of the Infantry Combat Badge is to include the motorized infantry regiments. The color of this badge is bronze.

The badge will be authorized through the regiment commander. The recipient will receive an award document and the badge will be worn on the left breast.

Regulations covering the Infantry Combat Badge: Army Regulations1939, Section B, Publication 82. Directive 27, p. 389; 1940, Section B, Publication 56, p. 379, No. 537; 1941, Section C, Publication 16, Directive 8, p. 137, No. 211; 1941, Section C, Publication 29, Directive 15, p. 303, No. 449; 1941, Section C, Publication 56, Directive 28, p. 583, No. 855; 1941, Section C, Publication 59, Directive 30, p. 619, No. 907; 1942, Section B, Publication 17, Directive 6, p. 154, No.261; 1942, Section B, Publication 49, Directive 17, p. 409, No. 687; 1942, Section B, Publication 55, Directive 19, p. 445, No. 760.

2. The Tank Combat Badge

(Das Panzerkampfabzeichen)

The Tank Combat Badge was established on December 20, 1939 by the Army commander-in-chief *(designed by Ernst Peekhaus, Berlin).*

The Tank Combat Badge in silver is awarded to officers, NCO's and enlisted men attached to armoured units that have since January 1, 1940 served as one of the following:

Tank commander
Tank driver
Tank gunner
Tank radioman

with a mininum of three tank engagements on three different days.

Through Army Directive of June 1, 1940, the award of the Tank Combat Badge will include rifle regiments, rifle battalions of tank divisions and tank reconnaissance units. The color of the Tank Combat Badge for the aforementioned troops will be bronze. The badge in silver may be awarded to tank signal battalions if the proper criteria is met.

The Tank Combat Badge will be awarded through the commander of tank divisions.

The badge will be given with an award document. The Tank Combat Badge will be worn on the left breast.

Tank Combat Badge

In bronze for rifle regiments, rifle battalions of tank divisions and tank reconnaissance units

Regulations covering the Tank Combat Badge: Army Regulations1939, Section B, Publication 82, Directive 27, p. 393; 1941, Section C, Publication 16, Directive 8, p. 137, No. 211; 1941, Section C, Publication 29, Directive 15, p. 303, No. 449; 1941, Section C, Publication 56, Directive 28, p. 583, No. 855; 1941, Section C, Publication 59, Directive 30, p. 619, No. 907; 1942, Section B, Publication 17, Directive 6, p. 154, No. 261; 1942, Section B, Publication 49, Directive 17, p. 409, No. 687; 1942, Section B, Publication 55, Directive 19, p. 445, No. 760.

3. The General Assault Badge

(Das Sturmabzeichen)

On June 1, 1940, under the same regulations as the Infantry Combat Badge, the commander-in-chief of the Army created a special combat badge for other combat soldiers. This would include the troops of the assault artillery who along with other infantry or armoured units as well as their own units who may qualify for the Infantry Combat Badge shall be awarded the General Assault Badge *(designed by Ernst Peekhaus, Berlin)*.

The award criteria for the General Assault Badge is the same as for the Infantry Combat Badge. The awarding of the General Assault Badge is made through the appropiate division commander.

General Assault Badge

Army Anti-Aircraft Badge

The recipient will receive an award document. The badge will be worn on the left breast.

Regulations covering the General Assault Badge: Decree: Special Printing of June 1, 1940, Army Regulations 1940, Section B, Publication 56, p. 379, No. 536 and 537; 1941, Section C, Publication 16, Directive 8, p. 137, No. 211; 1941, Section C, Publication 29, Directive 15, p. 303, No. 449; 1941, Section C, Publication 56, Directive 28, p. 583, No. 855; 1941, Section C, Publication 59, Directive 30, p. 619, No. 907; 1941, Section C, Publication 69, Directive 34, p. 703, No. 1052; 1942, Section B, Publication 17, Directive 6, p. 154, No. 261; 1942, Section B, Publication 49, Directive 17, p. 409, No. 687; 1942, Section B, Publication 55, Directive 19, p. 445, No. 760; 1942, Section C, Publication 39, Directive 21, p. 404, No. 474.

4. The Army Anti-Aircraft Badge

(Das Heeres-Flak-Abzeichen)

The Army Anti-Aircraft Badge was established on July 18, 1941 by the Army commander-in-chief. It can be awarded to members of infantry anti-aircraft defense units and army anti-aircraft artillery defense units.

a) For the platoon leader, section chief, and gun crew taking part in the downing a minium of five aircraft.

b) For crew members of the heavy batteries of the army anti-aircraft defenses taking part in downing of a minimum of five aircraft.

c) For the gun crew chief of the downing unit, even though he did not actually give the command to fire, and specifically:

1. Were company and battery commanders when half of the gun crew of the their battery have received the Army Anti-Aircraft Badge and who directed the action of the units that received the badge.
2. Were the gun commander when half of of the gun crew including the battery commander (comprised of three and a minimum of two) previously received the Army Anti-Aircraft Badge then he is also eligible for the award predicated upon his leadership.

The Army Anti-Aircraft Badge is awarded through the General of Artillery and authorized by the Army Commander-in-Chief. It can be worn adjacent to the General Assault Badge. The recipient will receive an award document. How worn: on the left breast; when awarded with the General Assault Badge, it will be worn to the left (from wearers viewpoint).

Regulations covering the Army Anti-Aircraft Badge: Decree: Army Regulations 1941, Section B, Publication 45, Directive 15, p. 359; 1941, Section B, Publication 67, Directive 23, p. 515, No. 812; 1942, Section B, Publication 49, Directive 17, p. 407, No. 686.

5. The Special Badge for the Single-Handed Destruction of a Tank

(Das Sonderabzeichen für das Niederkämpfen von Panzerkampfwagen usw. durch Einzelkämpfer)

The introduction of the Special Badge for the Single-Handed Destruction of a Tank was on March 9, 1942 established by Hitler through the recommendation of the Army High Command.

The Special Tank Destruction Badge will be awarded to soldiers who since June 22, 1941, as a single combatant with only close combat weapons (anti-tank weapons, rifle grenade etc.) destroyed an enemy tank or an enemy armoured vehicle single-handedly. For every destroyed tank a special badge will be awarded.

Special Badge for the Single-Handed Destruction of a Tank

In a single-handed attack against a tank during an assault which would usually qualify for the award of the Infantry Combat Badge and the General Assault Badge, the Tank Destruction Badge can be given. The required three assaults is waived. The Tank Destruction Badge can be worn with the other badges.

The badge consists of a ribbon from spun aluminum with two black edge stripes on which is a black metal silhouette of a tank. It is worn on the right upper arm of the blouse. Subsequent awards will be worn under the previous award.

The award is given upon the written recommendation of the battalion commander. The day of the award will be recorded in the recipient's personnel file. A certified copy of the battalion order will be given the recipient.

Regulations covering the Special Badge for the Single-Handed Destruction of a Tank: Army Regulations 1942, Section B, Publication 14, Directive 5, p. 117, No. 190; 1942, Section B, Publication 49, Directive 17, p. 409, No. 688; — Air Force Directive 1942, Publication 35, p. 1180, No. 2166.

6. The Crete Cuff Title

(Das Ärmelband „Kreta")

To commemorate the capture of the island Crete, Hitler approved the authorization of the Crete Cuff Title through the commanders-in-chiefs of the participating armed forces branch.

The cuff title "Kreta" is white with a golden border and has the embroidered script "Kreta" between stylized palm trees. It was awarded as a combat badge awarded to armed forces personnel who by land, air or by sea took part in the combat action. These are:

a) military personnel who on May 27, 1941, either jumped or were landed on the island. Also to the crews of the special transport squadrons transporting parachutists or those involved in the landing.

b) air force personnel who on May 27, 1941, participated in combat missions over the island or the sea in reconnaissance, fighter, fighter-bomber, dive bomber, or bomber aircraft.

Crete Cuff Title

c) military personnel who on May 19, 1941, in light patrol boats patrolled or took part in combat around the island of Crete.
d) naval personnel who up to May 27, 1941, participated in the capture of the island of Crete or took part in naval engagements in the waters off the island.

The cuff title is authorized through the High Command of the participating branches of the Armed Forces.

The recipient receives an award document. The cuff title is to be worn on the lower left cuff of the tunic (and also on the overcoat of all uniforms of the Armed Forces). It can be worn on Party and State uniforms.

Regulations covering the Crete Cuff Title: Army Regulations 1942, Directive 23, p. 457, No. 874. — Air Force Regulations 1942, Directive 40, p. 1403, No. 2519. — Navy Regulations 1942, Publication 29, p. 831, No. 721; 1942, Publication 36, p. 1000, No. 901.

7. The Africa Cuff Title

(Das Ärmelband „Afrika")

Hitler approved the authorization of the Afrika Cuff Title through the three branches of the Armed Forces.

The khaki colored camel hair cuff title has a silver border and has the silver embroidered script "Afrika." This is flanked on both ends by a silver palm tree. It was awarded as a combat badge awarded to armed forces personnel and non-military personnel attached to a military command who:

a) served a minium of six months in the African theater of operations, or
b) were wounded in action in or over Africa, or
c) contracted an illness in the African theater of operations which resulted in the inability to serve on active duty. However, three months service in Africa is required.

The award of the cuff title "Afrika" is not authorized for foreigners.

Awarding of the cuff title is through the High Command of the branches of the Armed Forces involved.

Africa Cuff Title

The recipient receives an award document. The cuff title is to be worn on the lower left cuff of the tunic (and also on the overcoat). It can also be worn on Party and State uniforms.

Regulations covering the Africa Cuff Title: Army Regulations 1943, Directive 2, p. 33, No. 60.

See Addendum No. 2, page 151, for Close Combat Badge.

c) Navy

1. The Submarine War Badge

(Das U-Boots-Kriegsabzeichen)

Submarine War Badge

The 1939 Submarine War Badge was established on October 13, 1939 through the Commander-in-Chief of the Navy.

It can be awarded to all officers, petty officers, and enlisted men who displayed courage in the face of the enemy on two or more occasions. This requirement is not applicable to those wounded in action.

The award of the badge is made through the Commander-in-Chief of the Submarine service. The recipient receives an award document. The badge is worn on the left breast.

Regulations covering the Submarine War Badge: Navy Regulations 1939, Directive 38, p. 693, No. 788; 1941 Directive 8, p. 108, No. 144.

2. The Destroyer War Badge

(Das Zerstörer-Kriegsabzeichen)

To commemorate the destroyer successes during the campaigns at Narvik and in the seas around England under the command of Commodore Bonte, the Navy Commander-in-Chief established the Destroyer War Badge on June 4, 1940 *(designed by Paul Casberg, Berlin).*

It can be awarded to crews of destroyers engaged at Narvik. On October 22, 1940, the Naval Commander-in-Chief authorized the Destroyer War Badge be given to crews of Torpedo Boat squadrons in recognition of their attacks against the enemy.

To receive the badge the following requirements must be met:

a) Participation in three engagements or three offensive mine laying operations or twelve war patrols, or

b) as a special award for missions in the operational areas or for outstanding actions, or
c) participation in outstanding actions under orders of the Flotilla Chief, i.e. commanding Admirals.

Destroyer War Badge

Those destroyer crews who were engaged at Narvik do not need to fulfill any other criteria.

Further the Destroyer War Badge can be awarded to:

a) survivors of ships sunk through enemy action, or
b) in special cases for wounded personnel.

The award will be made by the captain of the Destroyer or the captain of the Torpedo Boat.

The recipient receives an award document. The badge is worn on the left breast.

Regulations covering the Destroyer War Badge: Navy Regulations 1940, Directive 24, p. 393, No. 365; 1940, Directive 35, p. 730, No. 670; 1940, Directive 31, p. 606, No. 582; 1940, Directive 39, p. 808, No. 758; 1941, Directive 8, p. 108, No. 144.

The War Badge for Mine Sweepers, Sub-Chasers and Escort Ships

3. The War Badge for Mine Sweepers, Sub-Chasers and Escort Ships

(Das Kriegsabzeichen für Minensuch-, U-Boots-Jagd-und Sicherungsverbände)

This War Badge for Mine Sweepers, Sub-Chasers and Escort Ships was authorized on August 31, 1940, by the Navy Commander-in-Chief in recognition of valuable services rendered by personnel in these divisions *(designed by sculptor Otto Placzek, Berlin).*

The war badge can be awarded to crew members of these vessels for distinction and good conduct.

To receive the badge the following requirements must be met:

a) Participation in three engagements, or
b) As a special award for missions in the operational areas or for outstanding actions, or
c) Participation in outstanding actions under orders of the Flotilla Chief, i.e. commanding Admirals.

The award of the war badge is made through the decisions of the ship commanders. It may also be awarded to survivors of ships sunk through enemy actions, or in special cases for wounded personnel. The war badge is awarded by the captains of the mine sweepers and the captains of the escort ships and the rest through the next higher authority.

The recipient receives an award document. The badge is worn on the left breast.

Regulations covering the War Badge for Mine Sweepers, Sub-Chasers and Escort Ships: Navy Regulations 1940, Directive 36, p. 743, No. 676; 1941 Directive 8, p. 108, No. 144.

4. The War Badge for Auxiliary Cruisers

(Das Kriegsabzeichen für Hilfskreuzer)

In recognition of the outstanding contributions of the German Auxiliary Cruisers in the war with England throughout the world, far from their homeland and having accomplished the sinking of large losses of enemy tonnage, the Navy Commander-in-Chief established on April 24, 1941 the War Badge for Auxiliary Cruisers *(designed by Wilh. Ernst Peekhaus, Berlin).*

War Badge for Auxiliary Cruisers

The badge can be awarded to (and including crew members killed-in-action) those engaged in war activities. The awarding is done by the ship's captains. The award of the War Badge for Auxiliary Cruisers is given to crew members with proof of a successful long range operation showing distinction and good conduct.

The recipient receives an award document. The badge is worn on the left breast.

Regulations covering the War Badge for Auxiliary Cruisers: Navy Regulations 1941, Directive 20, p. 301, No. 247; 1941 Directive 8, p. 108, No. 144.

5. The Fleet War Badge

(Das Flotten-Kriegsabzeichen)

In recognition of the naval actions of the German battleships and cruisers in the war against England in all oceans of the world and far from home and causing large tonnage losses of enemy vessels and reducing the size of England's blockade. The Navy Commander-in-Chief established the Fleet War Badge on April 30, 1941 *(designed by Adolf Bock, Berlin).*

Fleet War Badge

The badge can be awarded to crews (including those killed-in-action and other qualified personnel) of the battleships and cruisers as well as other naval ships serving in the combat areas, which up until this time had no distinctive naval war badge. The awards are given for the naval personnel serving on the battleships and cruisers through the commander of the task force. For all other naval personnel the badge will be awarded through the naval headquarters by, at least, a Commodore.

Criteria for receiving the Fleet War Badge is proof of distinction and good conduct, and confirmed active duty on one or more war cruisers for at least 12 weeks. Other qualifications are as follows:

1. when the mission was especially effective and the individual displayed leadership or was killed-in-action,
2. survivors of ships sunk through enemy action or special circumstances of being wounded in action,
3. for participation in the two engagements by Iceland ("Rawalpindi") and Jan Mayen.

To crews of other vessels attached to the fleet task force, the Fleet War Badge can be awarded to those personnel on ships that were engaged in action.

The recipient receives an award document. The badge is worn on the left breast.

Regulations covering the Fleet War Badge: Navy Regulations 1941, Directive 20, p. 301, No. 248; 1941, Directive 25, p. 424, No. 373; 1941, Directive 8, p. 108, No. 144; 1941, Directive 23, p. 384, No. 343.

6. The Torpedo Boat War Badge

(Das Schnellboot-Kriegsabzeichen)

In recognition of the achievements of crews of German torpedo boats and the successful attacks against enemy shipping which destroyed many British war ships and merchant vessels, the Navy Commander-in-Chief established on May 30, 1941 the Torpedo Boat War Badge *(designed by Wilh. Ernst Peekhaus, Berlin).*

The war badge can be awarded to torpedo boat crews (including those killed-in-action and other qualified personnel). Criteria besides distinction and good conduct must include a minimum of twelve enemy actions.

Other requirements are as follows:

a. when the mission was especially effective and the individual displayed leadership or was killed-in-action,

b. survivors of ships sunk by enemy action or special circumstances of being wounded in action,

The award is made through the torpedo boat captain.

The recipient receives an award document. The badge is worn on the left breast.

Regulations covering the Torpedo Boat War Badge: Navy Regulations 1941, Directive 23, p. 382, No. 337; 1941, Directive 25, p. 437, No. 393; 1941, Directive 8, p. 108, No. 144; 1941, Directive 23, p. 384, No. 343.

7. The War Badge for Naval Artillery

(Das Kriegsabzeichen für die Marineartillerie)

In recognition of the achievements by crews of coastal artillery in successful air defenses, the Navy Commander-in-Chief established on June 24, 1941, the War Badge for Naval Artillery *(designed by sculptor Otto Placzek, Berlin).*

The war badge can be awarded to personnel in all grades in combat units (including those killed-in-action or who died from wounds). The awarding authority is through the Commanding Admiral or the Admiral commanding the Southeast Naval District

The qualifying criteria beside distinction and good conduct is the accumulation of a total of 8 points under the following system:

Torpedo Boat War Badge

War Badge for Naval Artillery

Qualifying actions:

a) Downing of an enemy aircraft by heavy, medium or light anti-aircraft batteries. . . . . 2 points

b) Participation in the downing of an enemy aircraft by several anti-aircraft batteries. . . . . 1 point

c) Unit anti-aircraft defense systems crews and crews of medium, or light coastal batteries or other defensive systems including light anti-aircraft battery crews.*

d) Successful actions by crews of searchlight batteries of 150 cm. or an anti-aircraft searchlight of 60 cm. who contributed to the engagement with night fighters. .1/2 point

e) Successful actions by crews through radar detection in pin-pointing enemy aircraft positions and notifying the anti-aircraft defense system which in turn downed the enemy fighter or bombers but not radar which was a part of the heavy anti-aircraft defenses. . . . . 2 points

f) Successful actions by staff personnel of anti-aircraft defense groups which contributed to the downing of enemy aircraft. 2 points

* Original text does not show any points. Ed.

The badge can also be awarded:

1. for outstanding performance in combat,
2. for meritorious leadership by officers assigned as section commanders and upwards providing no other badge as been awarded.
3. to personnel who have died and completed or partially completed the required criteria or if the death occurred after being wounded, having an accident or contracting a fatal illness while on active duty.

The recipient receives an award document. The badge is worn on the left breast.

Regulations covering the War Badge for Naval Artillery: Navy Regulations 1941, Directive 25, p. 422, No. 371; 1941, Directive 8, p. 108, No. 144; 1941, Directive 23, p. 384, No. 343; 1942, Directive 5, p. 154, No. 112.

8. The Crete Cuff Title

(Das Ärmelband „Kreta")

Reference the Army Cuff Title number 6.

9. The War Badge for Blockade Breakers

(Das Abzeichen für Blockadebrecher)

Through the ordinance of April 1, 1941, Hitler, in recognition of the determined efforts of the crews of ships who at the outbreak of the war were in neutral foreign ports overseas and were able to break the enemies' blockade of the homeland and return home, established the War Badge for Blockade Breakers *(designed by Otto Placzek, Berlin)*.

War Badge for Blockade Breakers

It can be awarded to crews of the blockade breakers and to other ships' crews who sailed under merchant flags and whose actions were considered being equal to that of the crews of the blockade breakers. The badge is awarded in the name of Hitler through the Commissioner of the Merchant Marine. For vessels in the military jurisdiction, the award will be given through the Navy Commander-in-Chief. The award criteria besides distinction and good conduct is:

a) the successful breakthrough of an enemy blockade,
b. for the sinking of an enemy ship,
c) under special circumstances when scuttling the vessel is in the best interest of the people the action was justified,
d) for survivors of vessels sunk by the enemy,
e) for special circumstances when wounded.

The War Badge for Blockade Breakers can be awarded if the above criteria has been met by merchant sailors of nations allied to Germany and those who served on German warships or German commanded vessels.

The recipient receives an award document. The badge is worn on the left breast.

Regulations covering awarding the War Badge for Blockade Breakers of April 1, 1941, through Regulations RGBI. I, p. 325 ff.
Regulations revising the regulations for the awarding of the War Badge for Blockade Breakers of June 28, 1942 through Regulations RGBI. p.635 ff. — Navy Regulations 1942, Publication 38 p. 1050, No. 960.

10. The Africa Cuff Title

(Das Ärmelband „Afrika")

Reference the Army Cuff Title number 7.

d) Air Force

1. Combat Flying Clasp

(Die Frontflug-Spange)

The Combat Flying Clasp was established on January 30, 1941 by the Ministy of Aviation and the Air Force Commander-in-Chief *(designed by Professor v. Weech, Berlin)* in recognition of accomplishment in air activities against the enemy .

The clasp is awarded in metal for seven different flying duty assignments:

1. for fighter units,
2. for attack and pursuit units,
3. for attack and dive-bomber units,
4. for reconnaissance, sea rescue and weather observation units,
5. for transport units,
6. for night-fighters units,
7. for long range night-fighter units.

All flying personnel are eligible to qualify for the Combat Flying Clasp, specifically those holding the following flying badges:

Combat Flying Clasp

1. Fighter Units.

2. Attack and Pursuit Units.

pilot, observer, bombardier, radio operator, flight engineer, aerial gunner, war correspondents and civil officials, members of engineering and navigation corps, who in the course of their duties took part in missions against the enemy. The Combat Flying Clasp for transport flyers can also be awarded to non-flying personnel.

The number of combat missions to receive the Combat Flying Clasp is as follows:

in bronze for 20 combat missions,
in silver for 60 combat missions,
in gold for 110 combat missions.

Upon the award of the silver clasp, the bronze clasp is not worn and is returned. With the award of the gold clasp the silver is not worn and is also returned. Combat missions in other flying branches will be counted towards the next higher Combat Flying Clasp. The criteria is that the combat missions must have taken place at least 30 kilometers behind enemy front lines or having contact with an enemy aircraft.

Through the State Ministry of Aeronautics and Air Force Commander-in-Chief, the pendant to the Gold Combat Flying Clasp was established on June 26, 1942 in recognition of outstanding actions

3. Attack and Dive Bomber Units.

4. Reconnaissance, Sea Rescue and Weather Units.

5. Transport & Materiel Units with Pendant.

6. and 7. Night Fighter Units with black lacquered laurel leaves wreath and:
6. Close Night Fighter Units same as picture 1. (Fighter Units)
7. Long Range Night Fighter Units same as picture 2. (Attack and Pursuit Units.)

in combat with the enemy.

The pendant to the Golden Combat Flying Clasp is authorized to be awarded in the field

by Fighter and Transport units:

a minimum of 500 front missions,

by Bomber, Attack and Pursuit units:
a minimum of 400 front missions,
by Attack, Sea Rescue and Weather units:
a minimum of 300 front missions,
by Reconnaissance and Night Fighter Units:
a minimum of 250 front missions.

The awarding of the Combat Flying Clasp goes through the Wing Commander and the Group command with jurisdiction of regimental commanders. The awarding to members of the flying units and the army flying units follows the Air Force Command and the Army High Command. For members of the Navy, the award is through the Naval Defense Command. The awarding of the Combat Flying Clasp to senior and higher ranking staff personnel is done through the channels of the Chief of the Air Fleet through Commanding Generals and the Commanders-in-Chief of the Army, Air Force and Navy.

The recipient receives an award document.

The Combat Flying Clasp is worn directly over the mounted group or ribbon bar. The wearing of an embroidered Combat Flying Clasp is allowed.

Regulations covering awarding the Combat Flying Badge: Air Force Regulations 1941, Directive 7, p. 93, fig. 137, p. 95, fig. 138.
Regulations covering awarding the Combat Flying Badge for Transport Personnel: Air Force Regulations 1941, Directive 50, p. 1082, fig. 1886.
Regulations covering awarding the Combat Flying Badge for Transport Personnel: Air Force Regulations 1941, Directive 38, p. 729, fig. 1231; 1942, Directive 18, p. 627, fig. 1115.
Regulations covering awarding the Combat Flying Badge for Fighter and Attack Personnel: Air Force Regulations 1942, Directive 21, p. 727, fig. 1318.
Addendum for the Golden Combat Flying Badge, Air Force Regulations 1942, Directive 28, p. 961, fig. 1744.
Addendum for the Combat Flying Badge for Night Fighter Personnel, Air Force Regulations 1942, Directive 34, p. 1147, fig. 2099.

2. The Anti-Aircraft Artillery Combat Badge
(Flak-Kampfabzeichen)

The Anti-Aircraft Artillery Combat Badge was authorized on January 10, 1941, through the State Air Ministry and the Commander-in-Chief of the Air Force *(Designed by Wihl. Peekhaus, Berlin.)*.

It was first awarded in recognition of proficiency in both air and ground targets. However, after the authorization of the Ground Combat Badge (see number 3) the Anti-Aircraft Artillery Combat Badge was given only for successfully downing enemy air targets.

The Anti-Aircraft Artillery Combat Badge can be awarded to crew personnel of anti-aircraft artillery

a) for multiple qualified participation on successful anti-aircraft activity against air targets,
b) for special recognition of leadership during action against air targets or for merit by troop commanders.

The award is given only to individuals.

The criteria to receive the award are as follows:

a) participation in the downing of an enemy aircraft. . . . 2 points
Downing of an enemy aircraft by anti-aircraft fire or blinding by searchlight so that the aircraft is downed is considered sufficient to receive the point count. To receive the point count it does not matter whether the weapons used are anti-aircraft, machine-gun, rifles or night fighters (this includes searchlight personnel).
b) If the downing is the result of a heavy Anti-aircraft battery or a light battery (without participation of any other batteries) the point count for the crews is . . . . .4 points
c) Detecting incoming enemy aircraft first by either the 150 cm or 60 cm searchlights by acoustical means (not electrical) and following the enemy target to another searchlight . . . . .1 point

To receive the Anti-Aircraft Artillery Combat Badge, crews must have a total of 16 points.

Special rules for awarding the badge can be considered.

The Anti-Aircraft Artillery Combat Badge can be awarded independent of the point count. Also, the badge can be awarded for single acts of distinction and for meritorious leadership in the rank of unit commanders upward.

The awarding of the Anti-Aircraft Combat Badge may be made to personnel of Anti-Aircraft Divisions, Anti-Aircraft Corps and

Anti-Aircraft Artillery Combat Badge

Air Force Administrative Command (for members of anti-aircraft artillery that are not under the command of the Anti-Aircraft Division or Corps.

The awarding of the Anti-Aircraft Combat Badge to members of the anti-aircraft artillery without the required points goes through Chief of the Air Fleet. In exceptional circumstances the request goes to the Air Ministry and the Air Force High Command (Air Force Personnel Office).

The recipient receives an award document. The badge is worn on the left breast.

Addendum and clarification to Air Force Regulations 1941, Directive 4, p. 37 ff., fig. 69 ff.; 1941, Directive 34, p. 590, fig. 954 (not including enforcement); 1942, Directive 15, p. 484, fig. 922.

3. The Air Force Ground Combat Badge
(Das Erdkampfabzeichen der Luftwaffe)

As a sign of recognition of action on the front in ground combat, the Air Ministry and the Air Force High Command authorized on March 31, 1942 the "Air Force Ground Combat Badge" *(designed by Professor v. Weech, Berlin)*. The award of this badge as an "honor award" is not allowed.

The Air Force Ground Combat Badge can be awarded to members of the Air Force having been in ground combat. It is awarded on an individual basis only to those in the most forward positions and being engaged in combat for a minimum of three different days. In combat, the weapons used during an assault can be either infantry or artillery or man-to-man in close combat. The assault is credited if the attack penetrates the enemy line. For the heavy infantry and artillery weapons, the assault is considered successful if combined with support troops which penetrated the enemy line. Counter assaults and counter attacks as well as scouting in depth are also considered if the assault is successful. Participation in a general assault with tanks, heavy artillery and heavy infantry weapons support (against bunkers, etc.) will not be a basis for the award of the Air Force Ground Combat Badge.

For combat with enemy aerial targets, the Anti-Aircraft Artillery Combat Badge will be awarded and not the Air Force Ground Combat Badge.

Units in combat against ground and sea enemy targets in combination with other units who are in combat against air targets (downing an aircraft), and who have been awarded the Anti-Aircraft Artillery Combat Badge cannot be considered for the Air Force Ground Combat Badge.

Air Force Ground Combat Badge

If the criteria has been met in either ground or sea combat for the awarding of the Anti-Aircraft Artillery Combat Badge, this badge can be exchanged for the Air Force Ground Combat Badge.

The awarding of the Air Force Ground Combat Badge for troop leadership is not foreseen. Commanders, etc. can only be considered for the badge if they meet the required combat criteria.

For members of the Air Force who have received the army combat badges (Infantry Combat Badge, General Assault Badge, Tank Combat Badge) they are advised to exchange these badges for the Air Force Ground Combat Badge. *See Addendum No. 3 page 153.*

For recognition of combat engagements which would qualify for the receipt of the Air Force Ground Combat Badge, the decision for the award comes from the company commander, battalion commander, regiment commander or the next higher authority.

The award is issued through the appropriate division commander as no subordinate authority under a division commanding general exists. In questionable cases, the decision for the award is made by the Minister of Aviation and the Commander-in-Chief of the Air Force.

The recipient receives an award document.

The Air Force Ground Combat Badge can be worn by officers as a metallic-thread embroidered badge and a regular-thread embroidered badge for enlisted personnel.

The Air Force Ground Combat Badge is worn on the left breast similar to the Wound Badge.

Regulations covering the award of the Air Force Ground Combat Badge, Air Force Regulations 1942, Directive 15, p. 479, fig. 921.

4. The Crete Cuff Title

(Das Ärmelband „Kreta")

Reference the Army Cuff Title number 6.

5. The Special Badge for the Single-Handed Destruction of a Tank

(Das Sonderabzeichen für das Niederkämpfen von Panzerkampfwagen usw. durch Einzelkämpfer)

Reference the Army Cuff Title number 5.

6. The Africa Cuff Title

(Das Ärmelband „Afrika")

Reference the Army Cuff Title number 7.

II. Proficiency and Activity Badges

a) Armed Forces

The Motor Vehicle Driver Proficiency Badge

(Das Kraftfahrbewährungsabzeichen)

The Motor Vehicle Driver Proficiency Badge was established on October 23, 1942 by Hitler in recognition of special driving abilities.

Motor Vehicle Driver Proficiency Badge

The Motor Vehicle Driver Proficiency Badge is awarded in three grades, Bronze, Silver and Gold to drivers who under complicated and difficult conditions maintained the upkeep and care of the vehicles assigned to them. The awarding of the next higher grade comes each time the same conditions are met.

Criteria for approval of the awarding of the Motor Vehicle Driver Proficiency Badge is as follows:

a) Activity from December 1, 1940 in the former Yugoslavia, Greece, Bulgaria, Rumania and the areas westward of the Russian border of 1940 (prior to the incorporation of the Baltic states by the Soviet Union), Finland, Norway north of the polar areas, or the areas of Lappland and the German troops in Africa,

b) Approval for receipt of the badge in the preceding areas under especially difficult conditions are as follows:

as motorcycle messenger . . . . 90 combat days
as driver of combat vehicles. . . . . 120 combat days
as driver of recovery vehicle type I . . . . . 135 combat days
as driver of command and supply vehicles
and recovery vehicle type II . . . . 150 combat days
as driver of supply vehicle to troops . . . . 165 combat days

Combat days also count while repairing under difficult conditions, for example:

driving under enemy fire,
especially on particularly long assignments,
difficult road hazards,
and especially under uncommonly difficult weather conditions.

The Motor Vehicle Driver Proficiency Badge may be revoked under the following circumstances:

a) Proven reckless driving, vehicle neglect, or repair maintenance resulting in premature destruction of vehicles,
b) A neglectfully destructive accident as a result of irresponsible driving,
c) Conviction of reckless driving over the prescribed speed limit and endangering the vehicle under his care.

In the event the Motor Vehicle Driver Proficiency Badge is reinstated the grade will be Bronze.

The Motor Vehicle Driver Proficiency Badge may be awarded to:

a) Army drivers,
b) Drivers (not members of the army) under army command,
c) Drivers (not members of the army) in the previously mentioned occupied areas.

The badge may also be awarded to the following:

1. Foreign volunteer members of the army serving in combat and those who have sworn allegiance to Hitler.
2, Foreign volunteers from the liberated Bolshevik eastern regions and freed prisoners-of-war as long as they are serving under German Army command.

The badge may not be awarded to military members of friendly nations or allied troops.

Entitled to the badge are:

a) Drivers of the Army,
b) Drivers (not members of the army) under army command,

Regimental commanders, etc. as well as commanders of independent battalions and other commanders shall determine, for units under their command, the combat days credit sufficient towards authorizing the badge.

c) Drivers (not members of the army) who served in the previously mentioned occupied areas.

The Motor Vehicle Driver Proficiency Badge may be worn on all uniforms of the Party (including all branches and sections) and state uniforms. On civilian clothes a miniature badge may be worn on the left lapel.

Recipients will receive an award document. The badge will be worn on the left forearm of the sleeve.

Regulations covering the award of the Motor Vehicle Driver Badge of October 23, 1942, Directive I, p. 631. Reference: General Army Regulations 1942, Directive 27, p. 545, fig. 977. — Naval Regulations Directive 1942, Volume 37, p. 1020, fig. 922.

b) Army

The Army Paratrooper Badge
(Das Fallshirmschützenabzeichen des Heeres)

The Army Paratrooper Badge

The Army Paratrooper Badge was authorized for paratroopers attached to the army on September 1, 1937 by the Army Commander-in-Chief. The award was given after completion of training and receipt of a certifying document.

In order to retain the Army Paratrooper Badge the recipient must be re-examined annually. Future qualification for the badge required six jumps in 12 months.

After the paratrooper was attached to the Air Force, the Army Paratrooper Badge was no longer awarded. The army badge has been replaced by the Air Force Paratrooper Badge (reference the Air Force Paratrooper Badge, figure 6). Former members of the Army Paratroopers may keep and wear the Army Paratrooper Badge.

c) Air Force

The Air Force Flying Badges and the Air Force Paratrooper Badge are qualification badges. They are only to be worn on the military uniform with the exception of the Pilot Commemorative Badge. An exception is made for the wearing of the badges on the NS Flying Corps uniform (by direction of the Minister of Aviation and Commander-in-Chief of the Air Force on November 8, 1940).

1. The Aircraft Pilot Badge
(Das Flugzeugführerabzeichen)

The Aircraft Pilot Badge was authorized on March 26, 1936 by the Minister of Aviation and the Commander-in-Chief of the Air Force.

Aircraft Pilot Badge

The Aircraft Pilot Badge can be awarded to personnel attached to the roster of flying personnel after receiving their aircraft pilot license. The same regulations apply to personnel wearing the badge on standby reserve of the Air Force. Under the current regulations the Aircraft Pilot Badge may also be awarded to army administrative officials and personnel of the Engineer Corps of the Air Force.

The authorization for the award of the badge comes from the Minister of Aviation and the Commander-in-Chief of the Air Force through the office of the Chief of Air Force Personnel.

Recipients will receive an award document. The badge will be worn on the left breast.

Regulations covering the award of the Aircraft Pilot Badge: Air Force Regulations 1936, Directive 14, p. 165, fig. 420.

2. The Observer Badge

(Das Beobachterabzeichen)

The Observer Badge (for Observers and Bombardiers) was authorized on March 26, 1936 by the Minister of Aviation and the Commander-in-Chief of the Air Force.

Observer Badge

The Observer Badge can be awarded to personnel attached to the roster of flying personnel after completing not less than five missions over enemy areas. If wounded prior to the completion of five missions, the badge may be awarded, or two months after receiving the appropriate qualifying documents. For personnel in reserve standby the criteria is the same. Under the existing regulations the Observer Badge may be awarded to army administrative personnel or members of the Engineer Corps of the Air Force.

The authorization for the badge comes from the Minister of Aviation and the Commander-in-Chief of the Air Force through the office of the Chief of Air Force Personnel.

Recipients will receive an award document. The badge will be worn on the left breast.

Regulations covering the award of the Observer Badge: Air Force Regulations 1936, Directive 14, p. 165, fig. 420.

3. The Combined Aircraft Pilot and Observer Badge

(Luftwaffendoppelabzeichen)

The Combined Aircraft Pilot and Observer Badge was authorized on March 26, 1936 by the Minister of Aviation and the Commander-in-Chief of the Air Force.

Combined Aircraft Pilot and Observer Badge

The awarding of the Combined Aircraft Pilot and Observer Badge requires a minimum of one year of having either the Aircraft Pilot Badge or the Observer Badge with the appropriate issue documents. Under the existing regulations the Badge may be awarded to army administrative personnel or members of the Engineer Corps of the Air Force.

The authorization for the Combined Aircraft Pilot and Observer Badge comes from the Minister of Aviation and the Commander-in-Chief of the Air Force through the office of the Chief of Air Force Personnel.

Recipients will receive an award document. The badge will be worn on the left breast.

In special circumstances Reichsmarshall Hermann Göring and the Commander-in-Chief of the Air Force has authorized the Combined Aircraft Pilot and Observer to be given in gold and with diamonds. The Italian Leader, Benito Mussolini, was awarded such a badge.

Regulations covering the award of the Combined Aircraft Pilot and Observer Badge: Air Force Regulations 1936, Directive 14, p. 165, fig. 420.

4. The Aerial Gunner Badge

(Das Fliegerschützenabzeichen)

The Aerial Gunner Badge (Radio Operater, Flight Engineer and Aerial Gunner) was authorized on March 26, 1936 by the Minister of Aviation and the Commander-in-Chief of the Air Force.

Aerial Gunner Badge for Radioman

For Flight Engineer and AerialGunner without lightning bolts

The badge can be awarded under the same criteria and requirements as the Air Force Observer Badge.

The authorization comes from the Minister of Aviation and the Commander-in-Chief of the Air Force through the office of the Chief of Air Force Personnel.

Recipients will receive an award document. The badge will be worn on the left breast.

Regulations covering the award of the Aerial Gunner Badge: Air Force Regulations 1936, Directive 14, p. 165, fig. 420; 1940, Directive 35, p. 485, fig. 989; 1942, Directive 27, p. 922, fig. 1698.

5. The Glider Pilot Badge

(Das Segelflugzeugführerabzeichen)

The Glider Pilot Badge was authorized on December 16, 1940 by the Minister of Aviation and the Commander-in-Chief of the Air Force.

Glider Pilot Badge

The badge can be authorized for army personnel attached to the Air Force after being certified.

The authorization for the Glider Pilot Badge comes from the Minister of Aviation and the Commander-in-Chief of the Air Force through the office of the Chief of Air Force Personnel.

Recipients will receive an award document. The badge will be worn on the left breast.

Regulations covering the award of the Glider Pilot Badge: Air Force Regulations 1940, Directive 56, p. 895, fig. 1635.

6. The Paratrooper Badge
(Das Fallschirmschützenabzeichen)

Air Force Paratrooper Badge

The Air Force Paratrooper Badge was authorized on November 5, 1936 by the Minister of Aviation and the Commander-in-Chief of the Air Force.

The badge may be awarded to personnel completing the required criteria and with proper documents.

The authorization for the Air Force Paratrooper Badge comes from the Minister of Aviation and the Commander-in-Chief of the Air Force through the office of the Chief of Air Force Personnel.

Recipients will receive an award document. The badge will be worn on the left breast.

Regulations covering the award of the Air Force Paratrooper Badge: Air Force Regulations 1936, Directive 47, p. 610, fig. 1491; 1937, Directive 20, p. 260, fig. 612; 1940, Directive 35, p. 486, fig. 990; 1941, Directive 34, p. 589, fig. 950.

7. The Pilot Commemorative Badge
(Das Fliegererinnerungsabzeichen)

Pilot Commemorative Badge

The Pilot Commemorative Badge (combined for pilots, observers, aerial gunners and paratroopers) was authorized on March 26, 1936 by the Minister of Aviation and the Commander-in-Chief of the Air Force.

The badge is awarded with an honorable discharge to flying personnel (including reservists) if discharged as a military pilot. These regulations exclude recipients of World War flying badges who have not held the badges the required length of time. The minimumal time necessary to qualify to receive the Pilot Commemorative Badge for active personnel, reserve personnel and World War holders of the flying badges, was four years. For all other personnel the minimum time required is 15 years. With an early discharge as the result of an accident or other condition, it is possible to receive the Pilot Commemorative Badge. In the event of death in an aircraft accident, the Pilot Commemorative Badge will be given to the next-of-kin. Under the existing regulations the Observer Badge may be awarded to army administrative personnel or members of the Engineer Corps of the Air Force.

The authorization for the Pilot Commemorative Badge comes from the Minister of Aviation and the Commander-in-Chief of the Air Force through the office of the Chief of Air Force Personnel.

Recipients will receive an award document. The badge will be worn on the left breast.

Regulations covering the award of the Pilot Commemorative Badge: Air Force Regulations 1936, Directive 14, p. 165, fig. 420.

B. The SA Defense Badge

(Das SA-Wehrabzeichen)

Through the following order on January 19, 1939, Hitler authorized the SA Defense Badge aimed at building pride and military preparedness.

> "In extending my order of February 15, 1935 and March 18, 1937 regarding the awarding of the SA Sport Badge and the annual retraining, I elevate the SA Sport Badge to the level of the SA Defense Badge and make it the basis for pre- and post-military defense training. I designate the recipients of this badge as the SA.
>
> Every German man at the end of his 17th year who qualifies for honorable service with weapons has the moral obligation to obtain this SA Defense Badge.
>
> The age group of the HJ *(Hitler Youth)* at the end of their 16th year should prepare to obtain the SA Defense Badge.
>
> Honorably discharged military personnel capable of military duty and to keep their intelligence and physical strength should become a member of the defense establishment, provided that they have not already been recommended for membership in the Party (SS, NSKK, NSFK) and become eligible for the SA Defense Badge.

The Chief of Staff of the SA will forward to the Commanders-in-Chief of the Armed Forces the performance record of the recipients of the SA Defense Badge. The recipient is solely responsible for submitting his records through the proper channels.

The officers of the Party and State have the responsibility of supporting the SA in education and in evaluating the documents of the recipient for the SA Defense Badge.

(signed) Adolf Hitler."

The SA Defense Badge, formerly the SA Sport Badge, shows a sword with point up atop a swastika surrounded by an Oakleaves wreath.

The SA Defense Badge is awarded after passing a successful examination. To retain the badge requires the recipient to maintain a clean record in National Socialism and annual retraining. The renewing of the SA Defense Badge by the recipient requires his being able to successfully complete the required annual exams. This requires only completing certain parts of the criteria.

The SA Defense Badge is, as is the SA Sport Badge, awarded in bronze, silver and gold.

The criteria for the award of the SA Defense Badge is, with the exception of the change of the age from 18 to 17 years, the same as required to receive the SA Sport Badge.

SA Defense Badge 3rd Grade

The Bronze SA Defense Badge is awarded to those who have successfully passed an educational and physical program.

The Silver SA Defense Badge is awarded to those holding the Bronze badge for five years and participated and passed the annual requirements and also having passed the age of 35.

The SA Defense Badge in Gold is awarded to those holding the Silver badge for six years and successfully participated in the annual requirements and are over 40 years old.

The physical fitness program is divided into three sections, gymnastics, defensive sports and agricultural field service.

The award of the SA Defense Badge is given in the name of Hitler through the Chief of Staff of the Senior SA leader.

The SA Defense Badge can be withdrawn from the highest SA leadership through political, criminal or dishonorable acts and also for not participating in the annual renewal programs.

The badge will be worn on the left breast.

C. The National Government Approved Sport Badge

(Die von der Reichsregierung genehmigten Sportabzeichen)

1. The National Sport Badge

(Das Reichssportabzeichen)

The National Sport Badge is a government decoration that indicates the recipient has achieved above average proficiency in gymnastics. It is awarded by the National Sport Leader through the National Sport Bureau.

The National Sport Badge is awarded in four classes, bronze, silver and gold, and also to war wounded and other disabled individuals. The National Disabled Sport Badge is silver with a golden wreath. The criteria required for the awarding of the National Sport Badge is that the applicant must have good character and be of German blood.

National Sport Badge

National Disabled Sport Badge

To qualify for

the Bronze National Sport Badge, the applicant must be 18 years of age, or not older than 32 years (women must not be older than 28 years of age), and successfully complete the annual retraining for five years.

the Silver National Sports Badge

a) the candidate must hold the Bronze Badge and have successfully completed seven of the required examinations within 12 months, and
b) after the age of 32 (women must not be older than 28 years of age), the candidate must successfully complete five of the required examinations within 12 months.

the Gold National Sport Badge

a) the candidate must hold the Silver Badge and have successfully completed seven of the required examinations within 12 months, and
b) after the age of 40 (women must not be older than 36 years of age), the candidate must successfully complete five of the required examinations within 12 months.

War wounded and physically disabled men who, despite their disabilities, successfully complete five different examinations and, being above average in the same class, may be awarded the badge in silver with the golden wreath (National Disabled Sport Badge).

The Austrian Sport Badge, having similar award criteria, and due to the return of Austria to Greater Germany, may be exchanged for the National Sport Badge through the National Sport Bureau.

The badge is worn on the left breast,

National Youth Sport Badge

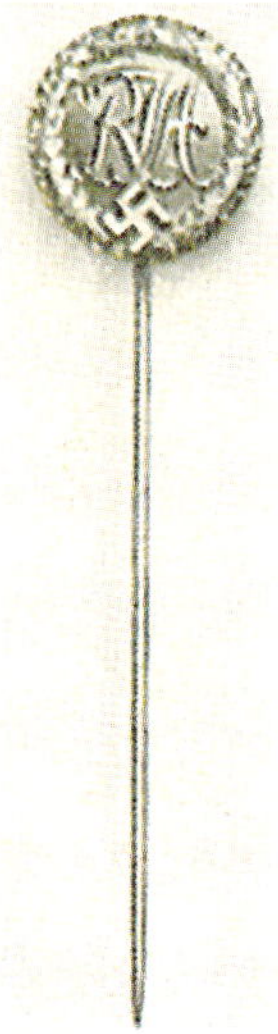

2. The National Youth Sport Badge
(Das Reichsjugend-Sportabzeichen)

To promote sport education in German youth, the National Sport Director has created the National Youth Sport Badge for German boys and girls up to the age of 18. The National Youth Sport Badge is no longer awarded and may be replaced with an equal decoration of the Hitler Youth organization.

The badge will be worn on the left breast.

3. The German Motor Sport Badge

(Das Deutsche Motorsportabzeichen)

The German Motor Sport Badge was authorized on February 18, 1938 by Hitler upon the recommendation of the Director of German Motor Vehicle Sports and the senior officials of the National Sport Administration of the German Motorist Association (ONS). The badge may be awarded to race drivers, long distance drivers and cross country drivers.

The badge shows an eagle holding a rolling wheel superimposed upon a swastika and surrounded by an Oakleaves wreath.

The badge is awarded in three grades:

the 3rd grade in Iron
the 2nd grade in Silver
the 1st grade in Gold

German Motor Sport Badge 2nd grade

The badge will be awarded on a point system. The Motor Badge in Iron will be awarded when the candidate has received 50 points, in Silver with 100 points and in Gold with 150 points. For the first prize in international races a total of 12 points would be given and the second prize would receive 8 points. For international long distance or cross country the first prize is 9 points.

The awarding of the German Motor Sports Badge will be held annually. The first awarding, authorized by Hitler, was on January 30, 1939 and presented by the Chief of the German Motor Sports and the Corps Chief of the NSKK.

The badge is worn on the lower right breast in either the metal or an embroidered version of the badge and on civilian clothes a miniature will be worn on the left lapel.

The recipients of the three grades will be registered in the Headquarters of the German Motor Sports and the State Minister and Director will present the recipient list to Hitler annually.

4. The German Rider Badge

(Das Deutsche Reiterführerabzeichen)

The German Rider Badge was authorized on February 23, 1937 by Hitler for the advancement of riding and driving skills.

The badge, worn without a ribbon, is a round silver badge which shows an SA man sitting upon a trotting horse and surrounded by an Oakleaves wreath which has at the bottom the symbol of the SA. It may be awarded by a State Inspector of riding and driving education when authorized by Hitler under the following conditions:

1. The applicant must have a minimum of one year as a Leader in the National Socialist Rider Corps (NSRK).
2. The applicant must be tested thoroughly in riding or driving proficiency by a State Inspector. The applicant must achieve at least a "good" grade to qualify.
3. The applicant must have successfully completed a course in riding or driving school and must have received at least a "good" grade. Attitude and comprehesion abilities as well as camaraderie will also be a criteria to be evaluated by the examiner.
4. The applicant must, providing he is not military, be a recipient of the SA Defense Badge.

German Riding Badge

5. Next to this badge, authorized by Hitler, no other riding or driving badge may be worn.
6. The recipient of the German Rider Badge will receive an award document.

Badge for Free Balloon Pilot

Badge for Motor Aircraft Pilot

If the recipient is dismissed from the National Socialist Rider Corps (NSRK) or the NS Party for dishonorable conduct, the German Rider Badge must be returned to the National Socialist Riding Corps.

The badge is worn on the left breast.

5. The National Socialist Flying Corps Badge

(Die Abzeichen des NS Fliegerkorps)

a) The Free Balloon Pilot Badge

(Das Abzeichen für Freiballonführer)

The Free Balloon Pilot Badge was authorized on March 10, 1938 by Chief of the National Socialist Flying Corps. The badge is oval with an Oakleaves wreath surrounding a balloon. At the top of the badge is the NSFK symbol.

The complete requirements for the Free Balloon Pilot Badge requires the proper documents in order to wear the badge on the NSFK uniform.

b) The Motor Aircraft Pilot Badge

(Das Abzeichen für Motorflugzeugführer)

The Motor Aircraft Pilot Badge was authorized on July 12, 1938 by Chief of the National Socialist Flying Corps.

The badge is oval with an Oakleaves wreath surrounding a flying eagle. At the top of the badge is the NSFK symbol.

In order to qualify to wear the Motor Aircraft Pilot Badge the candidate must be a member in good standing of the NS Flying Corps and a holder of the National Sport identification booklet for motor aircraft pilots.

c) The Large Glider Flyer Badge

(Das Große Segelfliegerabzeichen)

The Large Glider Flyer Badge was authorized on January 26, 1942 by the Chief of the National Socialist Flying Corps. The round badge has an enclosed Oakleaves wreath with the NSFK symbol at the bottom. In the center are three stylized white enameled sea gulls with wings extended.

The Large Glider Flyer Badge may be awarded to members of the NS Flying Corps and Air Force. In special circumstances, it can be awarded to members of the Flying HJ organization providing they meet the following criteria:

a) Qualifying Group I

Required studies and examinations:

1. Educational Preparation:
   Successful completion of flying classes prior to military education required by the Chief of the NS Flying Corps.
   a) Aeronautical studies,
   b) Aviation mechanics studies,
   c) Flying abilities;

2. Educational course in a National Glider School; successful completion of course to qualify for the Large Glider Flyer Badge.

Large Glider Flyer Badge

a) Qualifying Group II

Required studies and examinations:

1. Educational Preparation: Pilot license for Glider Class II;
2. Endurance Flight: Non-stop glider flight of a minimum of 5 hours flight time and return to the initial point;
3. Altitude Flight: Reaching 1000 meters three times in a single flight.

6. The Badges of the Hitler Youth

(Die Abzeichen der Hitler-Jugend)

a) The Hitler Youth Achievement Badge

(Das Hitler-Jugend-Leistungsabzeichen)

The Hitler Youth Achievement Badge was authorized during June 1934 from the Chief of the Hitler Youth Organization. The badge is in recognition of multiple achievements as a member of the Hitler Youth. It is in the form of an arrow, point upwards, with a swastika in the center having a border with the inscription "For Achievement in the HJ" *(Für Leistungen in der HJ)*. It is given in

Bronze at age 16
Silver at age 17 and older

On the official HJ sport shirt an embroidered version of the Hitler Youth Achievement Badge may be worn.

The qualifying examinations shall cover ideological education, gymnastics, scouting (field sports) and marksmanship. The testing results shall be recorded in the member's performance booklet which each member receives upon entry into the Youth Corps *(Jungvolk)* organization. This booklet will follow him into the Work Service *(Arbeitsdienst)*, the Armed Forces, SA, SS and others. Based upon successful grades and the completion of the required criteria, the bad-

Hitler Youth Achievement Badge in Bronze

Achievement Badge for the German Youth Corps

ge will be issued by the Chief of the Hitler Youth. The preprinted award certificate in the performance booklet will also be completed.

b) The Youth Corps Achievement Badge

(Das Leistungsabzeichen für das Deutsche Jungvolk)

Under appropriately reduced required criteria it is possible for youngsters between the ages of 10 to 14 to obtain the Youth Corps Achievement Badge. The badge shows a Sig rune for the Youth Corps and, similar to the Hitler Youth Badge, having in the center a swastika with a border and the inscription "For Achievement in the Youth Corps" *(Für Leistungen im DJ)*.

Golden Leadership Sport Badge

c) The Golden Leadership Sport Badge

(Das Goldene Führersportabzeichen)

In recognition of special achievement, the Chief of German Youth authorized the Golden Sport Leadership Badge in the summer of 1938. It is basically the same form as the HJ Achievement Badge with the addition of an Oakleaves wreath and is gold. It was first awarded at the 1938 Party Day and is worn on the left breast.

d) The Association of German Girls Achievement Badge

(Das BdM Leistungsabzeichen)

The Association of German Girls Achievement Badge is a rectangular bronze frame with the initials "BdM" (Bund deutscher Mädel). The frame is placed on a red, white and red ribbon.

The required criteria includes gymnastics, hiking, and knowledge of emergency First Aid.

The criteria must be accomplished within twelve months. The completion of the requirements shall be entered in the performance booklet issued each member. The badge is worn on the left breast.

BdM Achievement Badge

Young Girls Achievement Badge

Golden Badge
of the German Youth Champion

Badge
for 2nd Place Winner

e) The Young Girls Achievement Badge

(Das Jungmädel-Leistungsabzeichen)

Every young girl from the age of 12 must participate in the required programs for young girls. She must successfully pass the required examinations within one year after she commences the program. Along with sport examinations she will also be tested on general knowledge.

f) The Hitler Youth Champions Achievement Badge

(Die Meisterschaftsabzeichen der Hitler-Jugend)

1. The Badge of the German Youth Champion

(Die Nadel des Deutschen Jugendmeisters)

Under the auspices of the German Youth Championships all members of the Hitler Youth involved in sports must compete in the areas of annual winter, indoor, summer and swimming competitive games. This Golden Badge of the German Youth Champions may be won annually in each sport event by individual Hitler Youth members and BdM girls as well as by members of the winning sport teams. The second and third winners in the German Youth Champions will receive the same badge in Silver and Bronze. The badge has the inscription "Competitive Games" *(Kampfspiele)* and the title "Youth Champion" *(Jugendmeisters)*. It can only be awarded once a year in each sport.

Badge of the National Champion in Silver

2. The Badge of the National Champion

(Die Nadel der Reichssieger)

Besides the German Youth Championships, competitions in the various categories of gymnastics are also included. Under the National Championship compe-

HJ Marksman Award *HJ Sharpshooter Award* *DJ Marksman Award*

Award for Master Marksman
has a Golden Oakleaves wreath

titions fall contests that do not attract enough young participants to justify inclusion in Youth Championship competitions. This would include competitors under the age of 16. For those who have exceeded the age of duty in the Hitler Youth, remember the motto of the BdM, "Faith and Beauty" *(Glaube und Schönheit).* The first three winners in every competitive contest will receive a badge in Gold, Silver and Bronze having the inscription "National Champion."

g) The Shooting Awards of the Hitler Youth

(Die Schießauszeichnungen der Hitler-Jugend)

In 1936 the Chief of the German Youth Association authorized the Hitler Youth Shooting Awards. These awards were for the beginner, advanced and special classes. In 1938 the shooting badge for marksman was established by which the requirements went from 5 shots to 10 shots and also includes rapid fire at a field target.

With the large number of awards of these badges, it became necessary to broaden the criteria for the "Shooting Badge of the Master Marksman." The requirements were set so high that only a champion marksman could achieve them. These three marksmanship badges became so difficult to obtain that the youth did not participate in upgrading their awards. A hundred-thousand members of the Hitler Youth were holders of these performance badges.

The German Youth members also received the badges but they used air rifles to shoot at their targets. Already ten thousand German Youth members have been awarded badges.

German Horseman's Badge II. Class

German Horse Driver's Badge in Gold

7. The German Horseman's Badge

(Das Deutsche Reiterabzeichen)

The National Agriculture Association, affiliated with the National Association for Breeding and Animal Inspection and Control, authorized in April 1930 the German Horseman's Badge awarded in three classes,

3rd Class in Bronze,
2nd Class in Silver,
1st Class in Gold.

The badge is an oval Oakleaves wreath. Within the wreath is a horseman astride a prancing horse.

Each of the three classes may be awarded:

1. on the basis of special achievements,
2. on the basis of tournament events,
3. on the basis of racing events.

More difficult criteria must be met to obtain the higher class.

The Horseman's Badge is awarded by the National Association for Breeding and Animal Inspection and Control.

The badge will be worn on the left breast.

8. The German Horse Driver's Badge

(Das Deutsche Fahrerabzeichen)

Also from the National Association for Breeding and Animal Inspection and Control the German Horse Driver's Badge was authorized in May 1930. The badge is an oval Oakleaves wreath. Within the wreath is a driver in a chariot being pulled by two running horses. It is awarded in three classes — Bronze, Silver and Gold.

The requirements are the same as for the Horseman's Badge. The trotting race, however, replaces the racing event.

The German Horse Driver's Badge is awarded by the National Association for Breeding and Animal Inspection and Control.

The badge is worn on the left breast.

9. The Young German Horseman's Badge

(Das Deutsche Jugendreitabzeichen)

From the National Association for Breeding and Animal Inspection and Control, the Young German Horseman's Badge was authorized in July 1932. The badge is a round Oakleaves wreath. Within the wreath is a rider astride a prancing horse. It is awarded only in the Bronze class.

Young German Horseman's Badge

The awarding of the badge is through the National Association. Those under the age of 17 will participate in special examinations offered by the National Association, or any unit of the Armed Forces, the police, the NSKK, the SA, SS, and the State Riding Associations, which includes every riding and driving school and riding institute.

The badge is worn on the left breast.

10. The Performance and the Championship Badges of the National Socialist Association for Gymnastics

(Die Leistungsabzeichen und das Meisterschaftsabzeichen des Nationalsozialistischen Reichsbundes für Leibesübungen)

The Chief of National Sports in his capacity as Chief of the NS National Association for Gymnastics authorized these badges. They were awarded for top sport performances and for successful participation in sport events. These badges are awarded through the National Socialist National Association of Gymnastics as follows:

1. Bronze Performance Badge with or without year date,
2. Silver Performance Badge with or without year date,
3. Gold Performance Badge with year date.

The badge is in the form of a stick pin and shows the National Eagle with a Laurel leaves wreath (Bronze) and Oakleaves (Silver and Gold) sometimes with year date.

The Bronze Performance Badge with the year date is awarded for successfully completing competitions in one of the main sport events and can only be worn for the year noted.

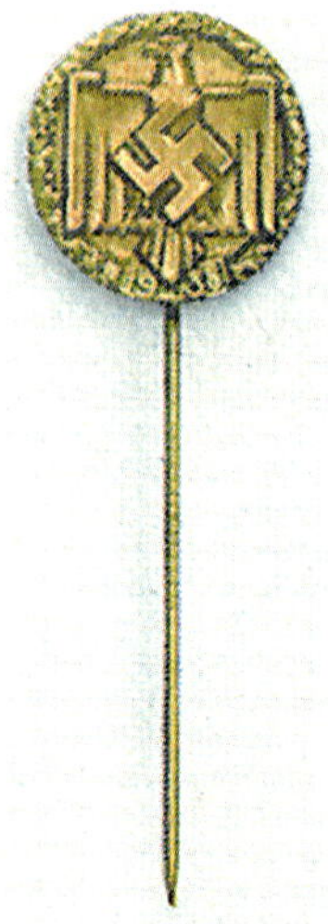

After the badge is received four times, it is awarded without year indication and may be worn at all times.

The Silver Performance Badge is awarded with a cloth badge for sport clothing in recognition of being a top athlete. The evidence of this status is

a) through participation in the final matches or those of the German championships in a single event,
b) through multiple representation of Germany in foreign county competitions.

When an "a" follows the award year, the stick pin badge and cloth badge may be worn until the next year's winner is announced.

When a "b" follows the award badge without a year the stick pin badge and the cloth badge may be worn at all times.

The Golden Championship Badge is also awarded in a cloth badge for sport clothes for the individual champion and team champions. The stick pin and the cloth badges may be worn until the next year's winner is announced.

IV. Legitimate Wearing of Earlier Decorations

(Die zum Tragen zugelassenen früheren Auszeichnungen)

A. The Decorations of the German Red Cross

(Das Ehrenzeichen des Deutschen Roten Kreuzes)

The German Red Cross Badge of Honor was authorized through the President of the German Red Cross on April 22, 1922; however, not as a national award. The last change in the design of the decoration was in March 1937 in adding the National Eagle. The eagle has on the breast a small white shield with a red cross in the center.

The Badge of Honor was changed to be the decoration of the German Social Services on May 1, 1939 by Hitler. It was awarded through the President of the German Red Cross with Hitlers' approval in the following classes:

German Red Cross Badge of Honor, Star

Medal of the German Red Cross

1. Star of the German Red Cross Badge of Honor (worn on the left breast),

2. 1st Class of the German Red Cross (neck decoration),

3. Merit Cross of the German Red Cross (pinback worn on the left breast),

4. 2nd Class of the German Red Cross (worn suspended from a mounted group),

5. Womans' Cross of the German Red Cross (worn on the left breast),

6. Medal of the German Red Cross (worn suspended from a mounted group).

Previously awarded decorations of the German Red Cross may still be worn. An exchange for the current corresponding class of the Badge of Honor of the German Social Services is allowed. Through the decree issued by Hitler on May 1, 1939, the previous awards of the German Red Cross can no longer be awarded.

The long service awards of 10 and 25 years service as a nurse in the Red Cross and the Golden Senior Nurse Badge in cross form are no longer honor awards in the sense of the decree of July 1, 1937. They can still be awarded.

B. Other Earlier Decorations

(Sonstige frühere Auszeichnungen)

From the former State and State-recognized decorations other than the decorations of the German Red Cross, these may also be worn:

1. Orders and decorations awarded by former rulers of independent governments or with permission from the former rulers up until November 16, 1935[1].

2. Orders and decorations awarded by the German government or the administration of former allied countries for merit during the World War, including the Silesian Eagle *(Schlesischer Adler)*, the Baltic Cross, Kärtner Cross and the Tirol Commemorative Medal.

Among these are included State-recognized decorations and awards given prior to and during the World War.

On March 3, 1918 Emperor William II established the Wound Badge; however, the regulations were revised on November 30, 1936. The revision was made without consideration to the number of Wound Badges or during what period the badge was awarded. The Silver Class of the Wound Badge usually awarded for three to four wounds can now be awarded to war combatants having lost a hand, a foot, an eye, hearing or damage to the brain. For five or more wounds the authorized Golden Wound Badge can now be awarded to war combatants who were wounded several times as above mentioned or were blinded or under care for severe brain damage. The Wound Badge of the World War may be awarded to participants receiving wounds in Austria *(Ostmark)*, in the Sudetenland, and all other regions that have been returned to Germany.

Through the establishment of Decree No. 1, these regulations also included post war legalization of awards given by former rulers of independent governments. This was desired by the various former States.

Also up until November 16, 1935 the awarding and wearing of the St. John Order is also and was allowed. In the armed forces the wearing of this award is allowed but not on parade or dress uniforms. New awards of this Order will not be allowed. (Also the Order of the Knights of Malta is recognized to be a foreign Order and falls under the regulations governing foreign awards [reference to "Foreign Orders" Part VI] and these formerly wearable awards will no longer be allowed to be worn.)

---

1 The effective date of this decree was from November 14, 1935.

The following awards and decorations are forbidden to be worn:

- the Kyffhäuser Commemorative Medal
- the German Field Honor Badge
- the German World War Commemorative Medal
- the Combatants Badge of 1914/1918
- the Prussian Commemorative Cross
- the Langemarck Cross
- the Bavarian War Commemorative Cross
- the Baden Field Honor Cross
- the Saxony War Honor Cross
- the Frontier Guards and Freikorps Badges
- the Austrian War Commemorative Cross
- the Emperor Franz Joseph Commemorative Medal
- the Keller Cross
- the George Cross
- the Schlageter Shield
- the Regiments Commemorative Crosses

Allowed to be worn is the Bremen Iron Roland *(Roland Ehrenzeichen)*, which was established in 1919 through the Bremen city council with permission of the provisional government for combatants who suffered heavy casualties during the liberation of Bremen on February 4, 1919 from the Communist administration. Special permission was granted through the Minister of the Interior on March 22, 1937 which recognized the provisional government of Bremen to be equal to a State government.

V. Honor Allowance and Honor Designation

(Ehrenzulagen und Ehrenbezeigungen)

With the award of certain military Orders and Decorations there comes under legal provisions or Order statutes honor allowances and honor designations. The most important are:

1. Prussia
   a) the Iron Cross of 1870/71,
   b) the Prussian Military Merit Cross,
   c) the Prussian Military Honor Cross 1st Class.
2. Austria
   a) the Military Maria Theresa Order,
   b) the Bravery Medal for enlisted personnel.
3. Bavaria
   a) the Bavarian Military Max Joseph Order,
   b) the Bavarian Golden Medical Honor Medal, which replaces the Bavarian Military Medical Order 1st Class,
   c) the Bavarian Golden and Silver Merit Medal, awarded since the year 1892.
4. Wurtemberg
   a) the Wurtemberg Military Merit Order,
   b) the Wurtemberg Golden Military Merit Medal, so long as they were awarded to Sergeants and enlisted personnel in prior wars up to and including the 1870/71 War.
5. Also for certain states, such as Baden, Mecklenburg, Brunswick, and Nassau decorations which authorized an honor allowance during the previous Prussian administration. An accounting for these rare authorizations is unnecessary.

The payment of the allowance for the mentioned decorations of old Germany was discontinued in 1923. However, in 1925 new regulations were enacted. Under the decree of Hitler on August 27, 1939 the stipends were reinstated. The recipients of the highest war decorations will receive an honor stipend of 240 RM (20 RM monthly). The higher honor stipends will remain the same.

		Monthly
Prussia:	Pour le Mérite Order	20 RM
	Golden Military Merit Cross	20 RM
Austria:	Military Maria Theresa Order	20 RM
	Golden Bravery Medal	20 RM

		Monthly
Bavaria:	Military Max Joseph Order	25 RM
	Military Medical Order 1st Class	25 RM
	Military Medical Order 2nd Class	20 RM
	Golden and Silver Bravery Medal	20 RM
Saxony:	Military St. Henry Order (Commanders Cross and Golden Medal	20 RM
Wurttemberg:	Military Merit Order (Commander) . . .	25 RM
	Golden Military Merit Medal	20 RM
Baden:	Military Karl Friedrich Merit Order . . .	20 RM
	Military Karl Friedrich Merit Medal . .	20 RM.

In addition to the highest war decorations with the honor stipend, as mentioned above, is the Grand Cross of the 1914 Iron Cross and the Grand Cross of the 1939 Iron Cross, the Knights Cross of the Iron Cross and the Austrian Leopold Order with the War decoration. All sentries with rifles will present arms to anyone with these honors.

VI. Foreign Orders

(Ausländische Orden)

In order to accept Foreign Orders and Honor Awards permission must be obtained from Hitler. By international agreement the foreign governments will request permission to award decorations to German nationals. The request will be directed to the Ministry of Foreign Affairs and they in turn will forward the request to the Minister and on to Hitler for final approval. The Chancellery will make proper inquiries regarding any political conflicts. If the class of the Order is proper for the rank or position of the proposed recipient and the recipient has no conflict of interest, then the Chancellery will proceed to get the approval from Hitler to accept the Order. The approval will then be returned to the Foreign Affairs Office which in turn will notify the foreign government. After being awarded the Order or Honor Decoration the recipient will also receive the acceptance and authorization documents.

War decorations (Bravery or Merit Orders) from German allied nations may be accepted and worn without obtaining permission.

Part Three

Wearing of Orders and Decorations

(Trageweise der Orden und Ehrenzeichen)

The manner of wearing Orders and decorations is regulated by the statutes (Orders regulations, establishment of the decoration regulations, presentation regulations etc.). These will explain or describe the proper procedures for wearing the Orders and decorations, i.e. over the shoulder, suspended from the neck, on the breast or from a button hole. Also if the star is worn on the left or right breast. Sometimes, but

Large Mounted Group

(1/2 natural size)

Ribbon Bar

not always, the authorizing statutes of the award contain specific regulations for the manufacturing of miniatures of a particular Order or decoration. For the armed forces and the police and for the Party there are specific dress codes which must be followed.

Decorations that are to be worn suspended on a ribbon from the right breast can also be worn suspended from a mounted group. For single decorations, they can be worn suspended from a ribbon. The earlier Bavarian type ribbon fold and the Austrian trifold ribbon are no longer permitted according to the current dress code.

Ribbons for long service that have embroidered symbols (National Eagle, Sig runes) created somewhat of a problem on the mounted group by the oblique way the ribbon must be attached. The symbols would slant and this configuration was not permitted. The firms who fabricate the mounted groups would improvise by placing a second cut of ribbon with the embroidered symbol on top. To avoid the appearance of a patch, the Orders Chancellery ordered a 5 cm. wide ribbon be attached vertically on the mounted group with pleats on both sides of the embroidered symbol which will open at the bottom where the ribbon is split to drape around the decoration. Through these requirements the look of uniformity is accomplished and the slanting of the symbol is corrected.

I. Armed Forces, Police and Official Uniforms

(Wehrmacht, Polizei, Beamtenuniform)

For the armed forces, the dress code of all branches of the services will be standard.

For parade and dress uniforms only certain Orders and decorations will be worn. These are:

a) German pre-war, war and post-war decorations, except the Order of St. John,
b) War decorations from former allied countries,
c) Honor awards of the National Socialist movement (see previous Part II p.71),
d) The SA Defense Badges,
e) Authorized Sport Badges (see Part III C p.118),
f) Foreign Orders.

When not on active service, other authorized Orders and decorations may be worn.

The dress code defines the manner for wear as follows:

a) Neck Orders:
the highest war Orders are worn above the peace Orders, arranged by free choice.

b) Decorations without ribbons:
at uppermost are the war decorations, wound badges, Silesian Eagle, Baltic Cross; next the honor awards of the NSDAP*, next the peace decorations, followed by sport badges.

c) Decorations with ribbons:
worn on the left breast in the following order from right to left:

1. Iron Cross 1939 or 1914
2. War Merit Cross with or without swords
3. Honor Badge of the German Social Services with swords on the ribbon
4. Medal for German Social Services with swords on the ribbon
5. Medal for Winter Campaign in the East 1941/42
6. War Merit Medal
7. House Order of Hohenzollern
8. Red Eagle Order 3rd or 4th Class with swords
9. Crown Order 3rd or 4th Class with swords
10. Austrian Military Maria Theresa Order
11. Austrian Leopold Order with the war decoration
12. Bavarian Military Max Joseph Order
13. Bavarian Military Medical Order
14. Saxon Military St. Henry Order
15. Wurtemberg Military Merit Order
16. Baden Military Karl Friedrich Merit Order
17. Prussian Golden Military Merit Cross
18. Prussian Military Honor Award 1st and 2nd Class on a black-white or a white-black ribbon
19. Austrian Golden Bravery Medal
20. Bavarian Golden and Silver Bravery Medal
21. Saxon Golden Medal of the St. Henry Order
22. Wurtemberg Golden Military Merit Medal
23. Baden Military Karl Friedrich Merit Medal
24. Other German Orders and decorations for merit in the World War in precedence of their class and, when the same class, by date of award.
25. Honor Cross for the World War
26. Austrian War Commemorative Medal
27. War Commemorative Medal 1864, Commemorative Cross 1866, War Commemorative 1870/1871

* *See Addendum No. 4, p. 154*

To wear the Traditions District Badges, they must be approved by Hitler. Recipients of more than one of these badges are allowed to wear only one at a time. Recipients of the Golden Party Badge are not authorized to wear the Traditions District Badges. It will be at the discretion of the recipient as to which badge shall be worn.

The Golden Hitler Youth Badge can be worn only on the HJ service uniform or on civilian suit coats and not on a sport jacket.

Through the special regulation of September 12, 1936, Hitler decreed that the Olympic decorations cannot be worn at parades or similar functions of the Party by members of the Party or Party affiliates.

The regulating authority for the wearing of the decorations and badges of the NSDAP is the Ministry of the Interior and is dated December 5, 1938. The regulation also applies to uniformed civil officials and employees in the National and District, Community and Community Associations as well as Foundations.

III. Civil

(Zivil)

For the armed forces, the proper sequence of wearing decorations is the same as for civilians. Separate instructions or official instructions regarding the manner of wearing Orders and decorations for civilians are not available. This is more or less what the regulations allow. The following regulations can be recognized as the proper guidelines:

Original Orders are only to be worn on special occasions. On such occasions the mounted groups and other awards will not be worn on the frock or tailcoat which includes, for example, veteran reunions, parades and other festivities and also on civilian clothing.

Grand Cross: The cordon of the Grand Cross shall be worn by high dignitaries over the vest [waistcoat] and at times under the vest. Along with the cordon the breast star is always worn; the breast star to the Grand Cross may be at times worn without the cordon.

Neck Orders: It is not customary, except for war Orders to wear several neck Orders at one time. The breast star which belongs with the neck Order may be worn without the neck ribbon.

Mounted Orders: The Orders mounted group may be worn on the

dress coat slanted on the left lapel. However, the Order sequence is reversed reading left to right and from top to bottom.

The large mounted group is not worn on minor occasions on the frock coat. In its place, according to the wearing regulations, the manner for wear on the jacket of the formal evening uniform for officers of the Air Force and the SS leaders is the small ribbon bar or a chain with miniature decorations attached without ribbons on which the Grand Cross, neck decorations, officers crosses and stars may be worn. Also allowed is a miniature bar which shows the proper sequence of the decorations. These may be worn similar to the large mounted group by being slanted on the left lapel.

For the manner in which the miniatures may be worn on civilian jackets, up to this time no regulations applied. Manufacturers and businesses created and offered the over-lapping bows of several miniature ribbons with swords and other metal attachments. One could see bows of six or more ribbons atop each other with several different metal attachments. Additional stick pins were marketed with excessive numbers of device combinations attached. The results were not in good taste and the standard became "More than what shows" *(„Mehr sein als scheinen")*, and direction was needed. Hitler's Chancellery had to supervise and regulate the business and fabrication of Orders and decorations (see Orders Chancellery). In agreement with the High Command of the armed forces, the following guidelines were created. These regulations applied only to miniature decorations being mass produced.

Metal Miniatures

(Verkleinerungen in Metall)

1. The stick pin or those miniatures worn in the buttonhole shall be the standard size of 9 mm. This guideline is approved by the Chancellery.
2. Metal miniatures are allowed only
   a) for war decorations of Germany, the former German nation and allied nations except Nr. 6,
   b) for the Life Saving Medal,
   c) for badges of the armed forces,
   d) for peace awards without ribbons (NS Defense Badge, Sport Badge). All other peace decorations may only be worn with their ribbons.
3. No more than three decorations may be combined. Exceptions are the Iron Cross 1st and 2nd Class and also the Life Saving

1. Knights Cross of the Iron Cross with Oakleaves,
2. Knights Cross, 1939 Iron Cross 1st and 2nd Cl.,
3. 1939 Iron Cross 2nd Cl., Spanish Cross in Silver with Swords, Life Saving Medal,
4. German Cross,
5. 1939 Iron Cross 1st Cl., 1914 Iron Cross 2nd Cl. with 1939 Clasp Wound Badge in Silver,
6. 1914 Iron Cross 2nd Cl., War Merit Cross 2nd Cl. with Swords, 1918 Wound Badge in Silver.

Medal. With these a total of four decorations will be allowed.

4. War Orders and decorations may not be combined with peace decorations or military badges or other badges except the Life Saving Medal.
5. Military badges of the armed forces and sport badges may not be combined.
6. The 1916 Merit Cross for War Help, the Austrian, Hungarian and the Bulgarian War Commemorative Medals are not authorized to be worn.
7. Allowed as single stick pins are:
   a) the Knights Cross of the Iron Cross with Oakleaves,
   b) the German Cross,
   c) the Pour le Mérite Order,
   d) the Prussian Golden Military Merit Cross,
   e) the Spanish Cross with or without Swords,
   f) the War Merit Cross 1st Cl. with or without Swords,
   g) the Wound Badge,
   h) the Narvik Shield,
   i) the Cholm Shield,

k) the Crimea Shield,
l) the Military Badges of the Armed Forces,
m) the SA Defense Badge,
n) the Sport Badges and other awards.

Ribbon Decorations
(Banddekorationen)

1. Ribbon decorations may be worn as a bow or bar as long as they are fabricated according to the regulations as set forth by the Chancellery. The bow must be made of only one ribbon. For ribbons of several decoration to be worn they can only be worn on a ribbon bar.

Bows

1. War Merit Cross 2nd Cl. with Swords
2. War Merit Medal
3. Army 25 Year Long Service Award

2. The ribbon that is worn as a bow must be 8 mm. wide and may not exceed more than 25 mm. in length. The bow will be constructed as a single fold and not a double fold.
3. Only the regulation metal miniature devices (swords, national eagle, Sig rune, etc.) may be worn on the ribbon bows. They must conform to required specifications as set forth by the Chancellery.
4. The ribbon bar may not consist of more than three ribbons. The maximum length of the ribbon bars shall be for one ribbon 25 mm. (25 mm. ribbon width), for a two ribbon bar the length will be 30 mm. (15 mm. ribbon width), and a three ribbon bar will be 25 mm. (8 mm. ribbon width). Regulations must conform to No. 3 as described above.
5. War and Peace decorations may be worn together on the ribbon bar.

Ribbon Bars

1 2 3

1. 1939 Iron Cross 2nd Cl.
2. 1914 Iron Cross 2nd Cl., World War Honor Cross for Combatant
3. 1939 Iron Cross 2nd Cl,. War Merit Cross 2nd Cl., with Swords, Sudaten Medal with Clasp

6. The Austrian, Hungarian and Bulgarian War Commemorative Medal will not be worn as a bow or on a ribbon bar.
7. Foreign Peace decorations may not be worn with German decorations on a ribbon bar. However, they may be worn as a rosette.

Miniature Metal Devices and Ribbons

(Verkleinerungen in Metall und Band)

1. The ribbon bows with attached Order miniatures may only be made and worn for the following war Orders:
   a) the Knights Cross of the Iron Cross,
   b) the Knights Cross of the War Merit Cross with or without Swords,
   c) the Pour le Mérite Order,

Miniature Metal Devices and Ribbons

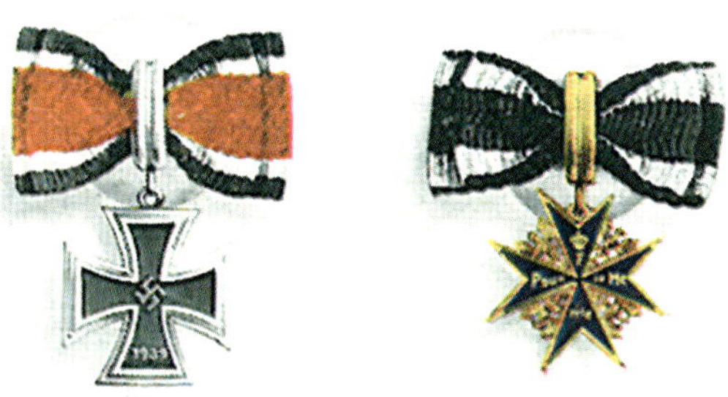

1. Knights Cross of the Iron Cross
2. Pour le Mérite Order

Honor Decoration for German Social Service 1st Grade

d) the Prussian Golden Military Merit Cross,
e) other earlier war Orders with special permission.

2. The Olympic Honor Decoration 1st Grade and the Honor Decoration for German Social Services may be worn only as a ribbon bow with an attached miniature neck Order but not as a pendant.

IV. Foreign Orders

(Ausländische Orden)

Foreign Orders — with the exception of war decorations — may be worn on special occasions, in honor of the specific nation or representatives, on the Order mounted group. Due to the lack of easy removal from the mounted group, the foreign Orders may be worn on other occasions.

Appropriate for foreign regulations, the higher foreign decorations, i.e., neck decorations, neck decorations with stars and the grand cross, may be worn from a small mounted group. The grade of the neck decoration (commander) will be distinguished by an attached rosette with the ribbon being the color of the decoration and silver braid sewn beneath the rosette. The neck Order with star (grand commander, grand officer) will have a gold braid on the right and a silver braid on the left. The grand cross will have a gold braid showing on both sides of the decoration rosette. Italian neck decorations (commendatore) are distinguished by the attachment of one crown to the ribbon. For the neck order with star (grande ufficiale), two crowns will be added and for the grand cross (gran croce) three crowns.

For foreign decorations to be worn on civilian clothes, a rosette will be worn. For the higher grades the appropriate braid will be added. These decorations are to be worn only on special occasions.

Part Four

Loss of Orders and Decorations

(Verlust von Order und Ehrenzeichen)

On January 8, 1943 Hitler established regulations regarding the loss of Orders and decorations.

The awarding of any Orders, Honor decorations and awards may be revoked in the event the recipient is found to have received the award through false statements or his personal character proves to be undeserving or unqualified. Awards may also be revoked if the recipient, through his later behavior, especially by a dishonorable*

* *See Addendum No. 5, p. 154.*

Penalty Regulations

(Strafbestimmungen)

Unauthorized wearing of Orders and decorations have always been punishable. The laws over titles, Orders and decorations enacted on July 1, 1938 increases the punishment for unauthorized trade in Orders and decorations as originally decreed on November 14, 1935.

Punishment of up to one year in prison or fine or both is mandated for the unauthorized wearing of German or foreign Orders and decorations or other honor badges. Anyone who wears, fabricates, offers, trades, sells, buys or otherwise brings into circulation fraudulent Orders or decorations will be punished. Also punishable are purchasing Orders or decorations without a valid identification or an authorization when buying them from a legitimate source.

Regarding the manner of wearing, no penalties are in force. In the event that the wearing of the decoration is not within the proper military or civilian guidelines (see Part Three) non-compliance of a service order will also be punishable.

Criminal conviction and loss of citizenship will result in the permanent loss of all Orders and decorations. The decorations and award certificates will be taken from the convict by the penal authority and sent to the proper administrative office. By the decree authorized by Hitler on May 3, 1942 as mentioned above (see military badges of the armed forces) the regulations against unlawful wear as well as the loss of citizenship includes the military badges of the armed forces.

Part Five

Orders Chancellery - Return Requirement

(Ordenskanzlei - Rückgabepflicht)

All requests and recommendations for the awarding of Orders and decorations must be approved by Hitler through the Orders Chancellery. The administration of the Orders Chancellery is directed by the Minister and Chief of the State Chancellery as the manager of the sovereign rights of the State's highest office.

The authorizing office closely examines the proposals and especially checks for the legality and details involved which must be correct and in accord with the guidelines; any questions must be cleared with the proposing authority.

Following the approval of the award by Hitler, arrangements will be made by the administrative office to issue the proper award and the award certificate with instructions for the proper wearing of the award. The Order and decoration with all the necessary documentation will be sent to the proper office for award to the recipient. For foreign nationals being awarded the Merit Order of the German Eagle, the request is sent through the Office of Foreign Affairs. The award of the National Prize for Art and Science is approved and awarded by Hitler personally. For individual awards, they will be given by the Chancellery.

The Chancellery is also the procurement office for all national Orders and decorations given by Hitler. This office also commissions the manufacture of Orders and decorations by firms in all districts of Greater Germany including newly acquired regions. High standards of quality control must be maintained at all times. In the manufacture of medals, the mints of Berlin, Vienna and Munich will be involved. In view of irregular demand, sufficient reserves must be available at all times. The concentration of procurement for decorations in one place makes possible the various decorations to be examined for form, size and quality of workmanship. This is necessary for the assembly of the Orders mounted groups.

The Chancellery office of Hitler through the Orders Chancellery administers the awarding of all Orders and decorations. They control and decide the manufacturers of all Orders and decorations. They also grant permission to market Orders and decorations and ribbons.

The manufacture of State Orders and decorations as well as miniatures may be fabricated and marketed only with permission. In order to maintain control against price lowering or reduced quality, the Orders Chancellery will provide a trained team of quality control experts to the Orders and decoration manufacturers. These experts will be responsible for price control and quality maintenance.

Responsibility to return the Third Reich Orders and decorations does not exist. After death of the recipient, the decorations will remain with the family as a remembrance. Upon the award of a higher class of the Merit Order of the German Eagle, the lower class will be returned to the Orders Chancellery. Although the loyal service awards, honor decorations and long service awards which are given in several grades, the lower grades need not be returned but may remain with the recipient.

The return responsibilities for pre-World War Orders remains in effect. However, war Orders need not be returned.

Addendum

(Nachtrag)

Addendum 1. Page 30 Include:

Awarding of the German Cross in Gold is allowable after having received the German Cross in Silver. If the recipient has been awarded the German Cross in Silver and subsequently received the German Cross in Gold, the recipient may no longer wear the German Cross in Silver but may retain the award.

Addendum 2. Page 94 Insert:

8. The Close Combat Badge

(Die Nahkampfspange)

The Close Combat Badge was authorized on November 25, 1942 by Hitler in recognition of those who fought the enemy hand-to-hand and also as an inspiration to fulfill one's duty.

The Close Combat Badge awarded for hand-to-hand combat is distinct and separate from the Infantry Assault Badge since the criteria is different.

The Close Combat Badge is awarded in three grades and will be worn 1 cm. above the mounted group or ribbon bar. When awarded the

Close Combat Badge in Bronze

Close Combat Badge in Silver

Close Combat Badge in Gold

higher grade only the highest will be worn. The lower grades will remain with the recipient.

The criteria for award is:

for the 1st grade (bronze)	15 close combat days,
for the 2nd grade (silver)	30 close combat days
for the 3rd grade (gold)	50 close combat days.

Criteria for close combat days are:

a) All combat days on which the soldier had the opportunity to be close enough to "see the whites of the enemy's eyes," use close combat weapons, to assault the enemy man-to-man and be victorious.

b) Also counted are days during which the soldier was a part of a major attack or assault, reconnaissance attack, defending a position, or a single messenger run, as well as an enemy reconnaissance attack.

c) The area — at a combat outpost in the front area, on the main battle line, at an artillery firing position, in the rear army areas (i.e. attacks by partisan groups), or an enemy attack on a hospital train or supply column, all are criteria for consideration.

Every soldier vulnerable to attack and on foot who gets into a position as previously described and proves himself successful, may anticipate being awarded the badge. The company commander makes the recommendation promptly and if possible the same day of the action by including it in the daily report. The commanders of regiments or independent battalions will record the close combat day for the unit in their daily log. The company commander will have a list compiled of the names of all participating soldiers. The list of names will be signed by the unit commander and be properly stamped. The authenticated list of names will be added to the unit's daily war record. Each soldier is responsible for noting his days of close combat in his personal military booklet (Soldbuch). From the platoon leader to the company commander on up the close combat days must be certified by the next higher authority. A duplicate will be kept with the individual soldier's personal records.

The close combat days will be counted beginning December 1, 1942. Counting of action prior to this date may be done under special considerations.

The division commander may authorize a soldier who being severely wounded with no opportunity to complete the required number of days, to be awarded the Close Combat Badge in

the 1st grade with a minimum of 10 close combat days,
the 2nd grade with a minimum of 20 close combat days,
the 3rd grade with a minimum of 40 close combat days.

For soldiers killed in action, deceased or killed by accident, the Close Combat Badge with the appropriate documents will be given to the next-of-kin. All prisoners of war and those missing in action lose their rights to claim the Close Combat Badge.

Awarding may be through commanders of regiments and independent battalions.

The Close Combat Badge may be worn on all uniforms of the armed forces, the Party, and may also be worn on civilian clothes as a miniature stick pin.

Regulations covering the award of the Close Combat Badge: Army Regulations 1942, Directive 28, p. 573, fig. 1030; 1943, Directive 4, p. 78, fig. 114 and 115.

Addendum 3. Page 107 Insert:

The Air Force Ground Combat Badge may be awarded to medical personnel when under the same combat conditions as set forth in the required criteria for assault troops, that being a minimum of close combat on three different days or being wounded or killed-in-action.

Addendum 4. Page 139 Insert:

The Golden Party Badge may be worn on the uniform. It must be worn on the uniform when wearing a small or large mounted group.

The Golden Party Badge will be worn on the left breast next to or above the Iron Cross 1st Class.

Addendum 5. Page 148 Insert:

criminal act which proves the recipient undeserving of the decoration. The cancellation of the awards will be voided only by Hitler. Hitler authorized the right to award war decorations to the Commander-in-Chief of the Armed Forces and Chief of the High Command of the Armed Forces. Each of the Armed Forces may revoke and withdraw any decorations or badges authorized and given by them.

Hitler reserved the right to revoke any Orders and decorations. All requests to revoke any decorations must be channeled through the appropriate Ministries to the responsible official in the Chancellery who then forwards the request to Hitler for his decision. When decorations have been revoked they shall be returned to the proper department in the Chancellery. Because of Hitler's right to revoke and withdraw, the Commanders-in-Chief of the branches of the Armed Forces must issue the required documentation.

The requirements of the regulations covering the revoking of decorations is also applicable to the combat badges as well as earlier-awarded German Orders and decorations.

Permission for wearing foreign Orders and decorations may be denied by Hitler especially if the recipient has not been deemed eligible. Permission denial by Hitler is also valid for officials and personnel serving in the protectorates. All requests to revoke any decorations must be channeled through the appropriate Ministries to the responsible official in the Chancellery who then forwards the request to Hitler for his decision.

Special requirements for Orders and decorations regarding those awards which do not require an approval of higher authority are still under the above regulations.